**Government,
Regulation, and
the Economy**

Government, Regulation, and the Economy

Edited by
Bernard H. Siegan
University of San Diego
School of Law

LexingtonBooks
D.C. Heath and Company
Lexington, Massachusetts
Toronto

Library of Congress Cataloging in Publication Data

Main entry under title:

Government, regulation, and the economy.

   1. Trade regulation—United States—Addresses, essays, lectures.
2. Industrial laws and legislation—United States—Addresses, essays, lectures. I. Siegan, Bernard H.
KF1600.A75G68   343.73'07   78–14159
ISBN 0–669–02664–6

Published simultaneously in Canada.

Printed in the United States of America.

International Standard Book Number: 0–669–02664–6

Library of Congress Catalog Card Number: 78–14159

Contents

Preface

This book contains texts of the presentations and summaries of the rebuttals and responses given during the 1978–1979 third annual discussion and debate series at the University of San Diego School of Law. The debates were recorded and transcribed, and the speakers were subsequently accorded an opportunity to revise their remarks for publication. Each debate constitutes a chapter in this book.

Government,
Regulation, and
the Economy

1

Industrial Regulation: The Market versus Government

Bernard H. Siegan and
John Kenneth Galbraith

Bernard Siegan's Presentation

My position is that federal and state governments should move to eliminate the vast bulk of existing economic regulation. By economic regulation, I mean governmental restraints on entry, price, and output. Economic regulation should remain or be imposed only when strong or compelling justification for it exists. Under this standard, a relatively small portion of regulatory controls would survive.

Mine is hardly a unique perspective today, although it once seemed to be in this country. In the years during and following World War II, market economics reached a low point among academicians and social commentators, many of whom were prepared to pronounce the death of capitalism and accept virtually any form of government intervention in the economy.

One indicator of this was the crescendo of invective and fury that erupted when Friedrich Hayek's *The Road to Serfdom* was published in this country in 1944. Hayek, a recipient of a Nobel prize 30 years later, warned in his book that economic regulation was highly inefficient and contained the seeds of totalitarianism. The strong opposition to his conclusions were in large measure prompted by lack of knowledge. For regulation was then still in its infancy in this country, and Hayek's reasoning was incomprehensible to those who, on the basis of hope and not experience, had been fervently preaching greater government involvement in economic matters. We now have hundreds of federal and state agencies regulating some aspect of private activity, and we no longer have to evaluate them on the basis of theory and hope.

Consider the case of the Civil Aeronautics Board (CAB), the federal agency responsible for the economic regulation of the airlines. If, during my undergraduate years in the forties, I had the courage to ask my political science or economics teachers why there was a need to regulate the airlines, the withering reply would likely have been, "Obviously to prevent exploitation of consumers."

Experience reveals how wrong that position is. We know now that rates for airline travel controlled by the CAB are far higher than those on routes it does not regulate. Many studies have been made of federal airline regulation, disclosing that its most significant accomplishment is the raising of airline fares. A study by the U.S. General Accounting Office (GAO) concludes that the absence of federal regulation of airlines during a 6-year period (1969 to 1974) would have resulted in fare reductions ranging from 22 to 52 percent. The lower fares would have saved domestic air passengers on the order of $1.4 billion to $1.8 billion per year.

CAB is not an isolated illustration. People all along the ideological spectrum who have studied the agencies are now aware that they are far from being guardians of the public interest and often have been created for reasons having little to do with the general welfare. Regulation frequently has been established as a result of a strange alliance between "do-gooders" and "do-badders," with reformers, motivated by what they deem to be the public interest, joining forces with businessmen promoting their own special interests. Thus very persuasive evidence exists that railroad regulation in the late nineteenth century, did not come about simply because of public outrage at the "robber barons." It turns out that most railroads supported regulation in 1887, when Congress created the Interstate Commerce Commission (ICC). They believed the ICC would help them impose an industry-wide cartel, something they had not been able to accomplish by themselves—and they were not wrong.

Fortunately, the unholy coalition of reformers and industrialists is becoming unglued. Friedrich Hayek and Milton Friedman have been joined by other distinguished company. Senator Edward Kennedy, for example, is now one of the leading and most effective opponents of federal economic regulation. Not exactly a free-market zealot, he believes that "the problems of our economy have occurred, not as an outgrowth of laissez-faire unbridled competition. They have occurred under the guidance of federal agencies, under the umbrella of federal regulation."[1]

Ralph Nader is another vigorous critic of economic regulation. He advocates economic deregulation of the transportation industry and removal of many other economic restraints. He has charged that "rate setting, entry restriction, merger permissiveness, technology frustration, political interference, delays, data deprivation, and incessant business pressure at such agencies as the CAB, FCC, and ICC cost consumers between $16 billion and $24.2 billion annually in waste and overcharges."[2]

Senator Kennedy leads in the fight for substantial deregulation of airlines and trucking and has the support of Nader, many prominent liberal and conservative groups, the Antitrust Division of the Department of Justice, and the President's Council of Economic Advisors. The White House supports airline and trucking deregulation. The former chairman, the present chairman, and all other members of the CAB favor large curtailment of CAB power over entry, fares, and routes. Even the CAB professional staff, which by all standards of Washington bureaucracy should be discouraging the effort, has instead approved of it.

The principal opponents of deregulation are most of the major airlines and their lenders. They are supported by the AFL-CIO and the labor unions connected with the airline industry. The pattern is not unusual. The regulated businesses frequently are the major opponents of deregulation. If, as pro regulators have been telling us for years, regulation is intended to curb industrial giants in order to protect the consumer, why, one wonders, are so many of these giants eager to retain the system?

Many other deregulation efforts are underway. In 1975, Senator Kennedy introduced in the Senate the Competition Improvements Act, reported out in 1976 in modified form by the Senate Judiciary Committee, a bill which one writer described as "so sweeping in its potential effect as to strike fear in the hearts of every federal regulatory agency, as well as the businessmen and unions hovering under their protection."[3] The measure was not acted on in the last session of Congress, and Kennedy recently reintroduced it. The more recent version requires five major federal agencies to promote competition and bear the burden in court of proving justification for action failing to comply with this mandate. Given the regulatory propensity against competition, the Kennedy bill might seriously limit these agencies.

In at least twenty-four legislators and in the U.S. Congress, measures have been introduced, dubbed "sunset laws," that requires state regulatory agencies to justify their existence at specified intervals. Lacking such justification, they will be abolished. This type of law originated in Colorado, where forty-one regulatory agencies were mandated to prove the need for their existence every 6 years. The popularity of such proposals along the entire ideological spectrum is strong evidence of the concern with which regulation is viewed.

On the judicial front, there also have been some notable blows leveled against regulation. In a suit brought by a consumer group and the AFL-CIO, the U.S. Supreme Court in 1976 struck down a Virginia law that prohibited the advertising of prescription drugs.[4] The Court, with only one Justice dissenting (Rehnquist), brought commercial advertising within the scope of the First Amendment's protection of speech and press. According to the Court, the Virginia regulation prevented consumers from obtaining knowledge about prices that were critical to their well-being. The opinion said that in our society, a consumer's interest in the free flow of commercial information "may be as keen if not keener by far than his interest in the day's most urgent political debate."

In cases decided last year, the Court applied the same reasoning to invalidate bans on real estate "For Sale" and "Sold" signs,[5] advertising by lawyers,[6] and advertising of contraceptives.[7] Largely as a result of the decision allowing advertising by lawyers, many legal clinics have opened throughout the country offering legal services to people of middle income who would not otherwise be served. State courts have become concerned about zoning regulations that prohibit people from living in places of their own choosing. The high courts of Virginia, Pennsylvania, New Jersey, New York, and Michigan have thrown out suburban zoning regulations excluding apartments or other housing developments—and this trend continues.

Nevertheless, regulation is not about to expire. Businessmen continually seek to impose regulation, presumably in the belief it is easier to outwit government than the marketplace. Kennedy, Nader, and many other liberal reformers still favor regulation where health and safety are involved—for example, in such areas as the environment, drugs, product safety, and working conditions. They are also proponents of energy regulation. Many conservatives support zoning and environmental controls. Clearly, experience still has not triumphed over hope. It was no different in Samuel Johnson's day. You may recall that when he heard of the remarriage of a gentleman who had been very unhappy in his first marriage, Johnson concluded, "It was a triumph of hope over experience."

The prognosis for regulation is indeed a poor one, however, if reason is to prevail. Numerous studies have been made of the regulatory agencies, measuring and evaluating their benefits and costs. As part of a chapter in a book I am writing, I have sought to summarize as many of these studies as have appeared in the academic and professional literature, exluding for editorial reasons, reports on minimum wage laws and current energy controls. I was able to locate over fifty such studies produced by more than sixty individual and institutional authors covering regulation of transportation, electric utilities, natural gas, banking, securities, broadcasting, food and beverage, zoning, occupational safety, drugs, insurance, agriculture, and eyeglass advertising. Over 80 percent of these reports favor either total or substantial deregulation of the subject under study, an unusually large consensus in the social sciences.

These studies show that while every regulation invariably accomplishes some good, the vast number fail a cost-benefit analysis: that is, overall the disadvantages outweigh the advantages. Invariably, the result is also that those of average and lesser incomes, those least able to afford higher prices, are the most adversely affected. The most common finding is that regulation raises prices, first by restricting the market from competition, and second, by imposing a variety of requirements on producers or sellers that increase costs. This wide consensus should dispel any doubts that the problem lies with regulation itself and not with those who administer it.

Let me comment on several of these surveys. I have already mentioned airline controls and would like to broaden my discussion to include regulation of such diverse areas as trucking, land use, and eyeglass advertising.

First, Trucking

The Interstate Commerce Commission (ICC) controls the supply of certificates authorizing truckers to operate within designated interstate routes. Although it approves of over 80 percent of requests for such operating rights, the ICC has in the past rarely granted permission for routes that will create new, direct competition. As a result, the owners of operating certificates for the most profitable routes are insulated from competitive pricing. This is evident from the value attributable to these certificates. Thus, in 1976 a large trucker who carried operating rights on its balance sheet at $976,000 sold them at public auction for $20.6 million. That same year another trucker sold rights for $3.8 million that had a book value of $450,000. A study shows that of the forty-three sales of operating certificates occurring between 1967 and 1971, the average rate of increase in the value of these certificates based on constant 1972 dollars was 13 percent. In addition, of course, the ICC allowed the truckers in question to earn a very impressive after-tax return on their investments in other assets, somewhere between 9 and 17 percent.[8]

I do not begrudge anyone the fruit of government's labors. The problem is that ICC regulation is intended to protect both consumers and producers, and the existence of such substantial profits discloses that one of these groups is not sharing in the government's generosity. If there were no ICC entry controls, anyone owning a truck could establish and operate a trucking service along any route selected, and the resulting competition would transfer the value of the certificates to customer's pockets. Some limited deregulation of trucking has occurred over the years, and shipping rates in the sectors affected appear to be roughly around one-third or one-fourth less than would be the case under regulation.[9]

Second, Zoning

My study of Houston, Texas, the nation's fifth largest city and the only major one that has never adopted zoning, indicates that its market system has made land use more responsive to people's needs and demands than would be the case under zoning.[10] Paradoxically, the best way to accomplish the usual statutory goals of zoning is not to adopt it. Because of the absence of zoning, rents in Houston are substantially lower; there is more growth and development, less urban sprawl and land waste, and possibly a more aesthetically pleasing and cosmopolitan development overall. Over 75 percent of the metropolitan statistical area in which Houston is located, referred to as the SMSA by the Census Bureau, is not zoned. This area has led all other SMSAs in the nation in the amount of residential construction for the past three calendar years. Yet it is only the nation's thirteenth largest SMSA.

Third, Eyeglass Advertising

Professor Lee Benham studied restrictions on advertising in the eyeglass industry. In 1963, the year for which he collected his data, approximately three-quarters of the states imposed some restrictions against the advertising of eyeglasses. Some states prohibited only price advertising, while others allowed virtually no information on eye examination or eyeglasses to be disseminated for commercial purposes. The survey found prices of eyeglasses to be substantially lower in states that allowed advertising. Benham estimated that such restrictions raised prices from 25 to more than 100 percent for what seemed to be the same quality of product.[11]

As these examples illustrate, regulation effectively imposes minimum price controls. Unfortunately, unlike maximum price controls, the regulatory variety, with its control of price, entry, and output, usually works. Those concerned with reducing prices should concentrate on deregulation. When people remark to me about the low rents in Houston, I explain that Houston has rent control—but it is called "no zoning."

Regulatory harm is not limited to welfare economics. The regulators are entrusted with enormous discretionary powers, which can be applied for reasons ranging from the basest to the noblest. Consider with me the extent of the regulatory power.

The CAB determines what companies will be allowed to enter the airline industry, where the carriers will fly, and what they will charge. The Federal Communication Commission chooses which of four qualified contenders it will license to own and operate a television or radio station. The Federal Price Commission (FPC) sets the price of natural gas in interstate use. The ICC controls rates for railroads, buses, truckers, and movers. Throughout the country, in cities containing hundreds of square miles, zoning authorities decide how every single square inch of land may be used.

Different people, regardless of how wise and expert they are, can decide these matters differently. Decisions arrived at for the worst reasons—graft, favoritism, or political ambition—can just as readily be rationalized as those decided for the noblest ones. Commissioners with a certain ideological bent can be as rigid and unshakable as those influenced by corruption. Important rules affecting great numbers of people can be created purely by chance, depending on the voting mixture of the day. The rule or certainty of law, the individual's most important defense against arbitrary power, is a severe casualty of the administrative process. As has been said in the zoning context, when these commissions "flit about sprinkling golden showers here rather than there, they make millionaires of some and social reformers of others."[12]

Legislatures often allow the agencies they establish to exercise wide discretionary powers. This makes lawmaking simpler and quicker because the solons can thereby leave it to the agencies to resolve difficult matters. Moreover, agencies are on the firing line and will have to resolve, on a day-to-day basis, issues which the lawmakers can not anticipate. The result, however, is that the representative process is removed from a large area of decision making. With the advent of administrative agencies, the theory that a knowledgeable and understanding electorate would rule wisely and well, elect the ablest and throw out the rascals, became inoperative in a vast portion of political life. Agency officials with far-reaching powers do not have to submit themselves to the approval of the public on whose behalf they rule, and even though their executive and legislative superiors do, the gap between the public will and the exercise of authority is immense.

As I have indicated, regulation frequently protects existing businesses against the entry of competing ones. Not only is this power one that can be readily abused, but it also has a crushing impact on creative and imaginative people in our society. Bans on entry severely impede the opportunity for energetic, ingenious, and imaginative people to succeed by providing or creating something new or better for society. Consider some examples of what I mean. In 1967 World Airways applied for permission to provide coast-to-coast air service at a cost of approximately $79. The then existing fare was $145. The CAB held the application for about 6 years without ever setting a date to hear it. Then the Board dismissed it, claiming it was out of date. It took Freddie Laker 6 years to obtain permission to provide round trip air service from New York to London at a fare of under $300. Now Pan American, TWA, and British Airways offer competitive service at the same price. One can now fly Los Angeles to London, round trip, for $400. Laker's breakthrough has created a price revolution in international travel.

Admittedly, the World Airways dismissal was an unusual decision. Often in regulation the same outcome results only after extensive hearings, requiring the employment of lawyers and experts at huge cost. The regulators are more prone to hang the applicant after giving him a scrupulously fair and very expensive trial. The number of trunkline carriers that have been licensed since the passage of the act creating the CAB in 1938 is exactly zero, and this during a period in which the industry has grown several hundredfold, with many changes in board membership. A Senate report found that seventy-nine different firms had applied between 1950 and 1974 to offer domestic trunkline service.[13] Such practices exist because regulation is supposed to restrict entry and output. Thus, although its structure differs, zoning regulations continually prevent developers from building multifamily and average priced single-family housing for which there is great demand. The process itself inhibits entry. The cost and length of regulatory procedures and hearings have been so great that many potential applicants cannot afford the struggle and simply do not apply. Unfortunately, not many have the stamina of Freddie Laker.

Alfred Kahn, when he was chairman of the CAB, raised a critical question on the role of regulation in a society committed to individual freedom. He said, "If some businessman or woman wants to carry horses from Miami to Maine, and he or she has a plane, [or] there is somebody who wants to ship the horses, why in God's name do they have to come to me for permission? And yet, I spend my days, a large part of them, doing things you wouldn't believe, that are insane, that my Mother didn't bring me up to do."[13]

There are times in every organized society when freedom has to be limited. We pride ourselves in this country on believing that restraints on individual freedom are imposed only when exceedingly strong and sufficient justification exists for such action. Our Constitution and Bill of Rights are intended to protect us against arbitrary and capricious designs of government. In the case posed by Mr. Kahn, no plausible reason exists for curtailing the shipper's freedom because society is not benefited by the existence of a CAB. The same holds true for most economic regulation. A great many of us are being required to obtain government permission simply to be able to pursue our lives and livelihoods, even when the justification, if not insane, is at best remote and conjectural. This is not how a free society should function.

John Kenneth Galbraith's Presentation

You must allow me to say that I am not going to disagree across the board with Bernard Siegan, only where he was wrong. If he had taken the additional step of making a distinction between wise regulation and unwise regulation, I would have very little difficulty and very little reason for being here this evening. He says, in effect, that in this Republic, the most vigorous free enterpriser becomes a socialist, or at least a vigorous advocate of social regulation, the moment his bankers tell him to go to Washington to get help or his instincts tell him that he needs some help on his prices or a subsidy. This I think is so. By my calculation it took the steel industry only one month in 1976 to change its advertising from a demand for greater freedom from government regulation and big government to a demand for more big government. This happened when its profits receded and support to its prices and freedom from Japanese competition was indicated.

I also have sympathy with my friend on some other matters. To convey the impression that advertising is truthful seems to me a damaging thing. It is much better to have people believe that it is normally slightly fraudulent and be so warned. There should be no false presumption arising from government regulation that there is some integrity in this particular art. However, we probably should be a little careful where claims for lethal drugs or damaging narcotics are concerned.

On the other hand, I would hope that I might be able to persuade Professor Siegan that there are many forms of economic activity that have an external effect on the lives and well-being of *other* people; that this is so when one man's urban sprawl becomes another man's eyesore. Thus it seems to me that a well-zoned city like San Diego is an infinitely better place to live than Houston and accords no less liberty to its inhabitants. (You will notice the skill with which I get local pride on my side.) I would hope we might also persuade Professor Siegan that there is a large range of such activity where the larger interest—the more general liberty—requires control (and it will certainly always be imperfect control) over the lesser and more specific interest. I grew up on the banks of Lake Erie. During my youth there, it was a charming lake that smelled well, and the fishing was excellent. A lot of people from Detroit, Windsor, and Buffalo enjoyed the shoreline. In time, the effluent from Detroit and other cities came into the lake and settled to the bottom. The fish disappeared, the fragrance was palpable, and the pleasure that hundreds and thousands and tens of thousands of people had derived from that body of water diminished—an assault on their liberty. Regulation then arrested this process. The last time I was there, it was visibly more pleasant, and—although I did not consult them—I imagine that this was so also from the point of view of the fish. A general enlargement of pleasure and freedom.

I hope that I will be able to persuade my friend that there is a wide range of regulation that is of this sort. There is also a broad historical current here with which we must contend and which we must face. When I was first experiencing the not eternal verities of economics some 40 years ago, one spoke then as one does now of a crisis. This was a much graver crisis than anything you have experienced. In the 1930s things were far less pleasant, even along this lovely coast, than they are today. In the country at large a quarter of the labor force was out of work and farmers' assets were less than their liabilities; farming was in fact insolvent. By 1933, some 9,000 banks had failed, something that happens even today in San Diego, but not in quite such numbers. A hundred thousand small business firms had disappeared. None of this enlarged freedom.

There had been an underlying change in economic life which had rendered invalid some of the truths that had previously been taught and accepted. Change, among other things, had rendered invalid Say's law, one of the great economic clichés, which had held that there could not be a shortage of purchasing power. Production would always generate the purchasing power by which the current product could be sold. In the years of the Great Depression, when the great men of economics were asked what should be done about it, they counseled patience and warned against untried experiments (although experiments are usually of that sort). Or, since there had been a very severe inflation in World War I, they warned against inflation. But as that very dismal decade wore along, it became evident that there had been great institutional changes that economic policy had not accomodated. There could be savings in excess of investment. This, with Keynes, led on to the notion that the state, exercising a vital regulatory function, could prop up the economy, could supplement the purchasing power that would otherwise be deficient, and could hold the economy at or near full employment. This, in time, became an accepted economic policy in all the industrial countries. A Republican president even came eventually to say one afternoon, in a careless moment, that "we are all Keynesians now." This regulation, the management of aggregate demand, as we have come to call it, led, after World War II, in all the industrial countries to 20 years of extraordinarily good economic performance. These were wonderful years to be an economist. Prices were relatively stable, unemployment was small, and we took the credit for it. An absolutely marvelous period in the life of my profession.

Alas, it is my view that these years are over, that we have now entered yet another phase in which, among other things, it is not nearly so pleasant to be an economist. And it is one in which, to the dismay of many economists—and I think possibly to the slight dissatisfaction of my distinguished friend here this evening—we are faced, whether we like it or not, with a very large further thrust in government intervention. So, far from moving toward deregulation, we are going the other way.

The Keynesian revolution was, in one respect at least, a mild thing; it propped up the economy, but it left market forces operating as before. There was nothing in the Keynesian revolution that required governments (some action on wages possibly apart) to intervene in the way markets worked. Now in these last decades there has been an exceptionally profound change in the way in which markets function or, more precisely, in the way in which they do not function. Through the modern industrial society there has been a great effort by people to get some control over the income and the prices that they receive. The market as an impersonal force determining prices and incomes is very much beloved in the textbook, but it appears to a very large number of people as a tyranny, an impersonal tyranny from which they seek to escape. How do they seek to escape it?

Perhaps the most notable escape is one to which Professor Siegan has alluded, the modern business enterprise, particularly the modern large business enterprise. A thousand or so large corporations now produce somewhere around half of all private product. In that half there is a very substantial authority over the prices charged. Where we have large corporations, almost invariably—the exceptions can be dismissed—we have strong unions. The coming together of workers to exercise some control over their incomes is the purpose of a union. Where we do not have unions, we have a substitute in the form of a legislated minimum wage. Where we do not have large corporations, such as in agriculture, we have an association between agriculture and the government and the setting of minimum prices—support prices. And we have, as even my most orthodox colleagues would agree, a very large public sector called the nonmarket sector. Schools, highways, health services, and the common defense are largely out of the market system, largely subject to the political process both in the setting of prices and in the setting of incomes.

This is now the structural change for which an accomodation is in the making. However one might wish for the romantic world of Professor Siegan and his beloved onetime colleagues at the University of Chicago, we are not going to have it. In the world in which we live, when we seek by the older, milder Keynesian methods of fiscal and monetary regulation to arrest the process by which people seek more income and by which corporations then pass the higher income claims on to the public, we do not stop the upward thrust. Instead we produce slack in plant capacity and we create unemployment, and only when that slack and unemployment are substantial does the pressure of wages on prices and prices on wages abate. All this is to say that we have a choice among inflation, unemployment to control the inflation, or some direct regulations to limit the upward thrust in prices and incomes—an incomes and prices policy. Thus underlying circumstances and change are forcing another large area of government intervention and activity. If people must choose among continuing inflation and the continuing hurt that this has for many people, unemployment with the very large damage that this has for a smaller number of people, or an effort to intervene, most will accept the last. It is not something that one would want to do for its own sake. But in economics one finds one's self invariable involved in selecting the lesser of evils.

This is the direction, quite apart from preference, in which we are headed. Mr. Carter, to his enormous credit, brought five economics Ph.D.s into his Cabinet or at Cabinet level, and nobody will suggest that, however badly they are doing, they are not an improvement over lawyers. But they have not been doing very well. In the year and three months they have been there, they have slightly reduced the amount of unemployment, although it is still appallingly high in the central cities and for minorities. In addition, they have very substantially increased the rate of inflation. Moreover, they cannot be for inflation, and they cannot be for unemployment. So as it becomes evident that God is not a Keynesian Democrat, there remains only to decide how you intervene in the income-price bargain—how you develop a prices and incomes policy that allows you to prevent inflation without resorting to unemployment and that will not too much arouse George Meany. So more not less regulation.

I hate to cause distress for my good and learned colleague in this debate. I do not want to make him feel badly. But he must realize that so far from moving to a paradise of no regulation, we are almost certainly moving in the other direction. I have great admiration for my friend Edward Kennedy. He has seized upon the idea of deregulation of the airlines. But as a practical man, he will, I judge, be willing to accept that in the much larger area I have described and much as we might wish it to the contrary, more regulation is probably inevitable.

I appear before you this evening, I must say, in a mood for which I can only apologize. I sat enchanted, admiring of the idealism and romance that Professor Siegan brought to you in the picture of the brilliant return to the unregulated market society. But I warn you, tomorrow is coming. You will be right back with the untidy world of Galbraith.

Bernard Siegan's Rebuttal

I admit it, we are romantics at the University of Chicago, but I have some unpleasant news for Professor Galbraith: romance is reaching out to Harvard. Professors (in the Economics Department, no less) have turned to romanticism. They accept the kind of approach that I have been talking about. I read an article recently in this vein in Harvard's *Review of Economics and Statistics*—and it was not by Lord Byron. The author came to the conclusion (can you imagine at Harvard?) that minimum wage laws cause a loss of employment. So our romantic monopoly at the University of Chicago is rapidly disappearing. It has not only entered Harvard, but it proliferates elsewhere. A large amount of academic research now concludes that regulation does not work. These researchers do not say "Throw the whole thing out, get rid of everything," but they do make a very convincing case that instead of protecting us, most of the regulatory agencies are exploiting us, and that we should be guided accordingly.

Now it may be that someone will pass this research off and say, "What nonsense, these bunch of romantics." It's possible, but it would be very unfortunate if in our society of reason we dismiss testimony of this nature. The evidence is extremely strong that regulation does not work. Now this does not mean we throw out the police department, we get rid of everything, but it does tell us that we have got to start looking at these agencies very carefully. Regulation should not be imposed or increased without extremely cogent, compelling reasons. In view of the information we now have on the subject, I do not know what other course a rational society can follow. The evidence has persuaded people who were once convinced that regulation generally works. Professor Galbraith's friend, Senator Kennedy, is not one that goes around extolling University of Chicago economics, but he and many others on his side of the ideological spectrum preach about the same line with respect to much economic regulation.

Professor Galbraith advocates economic policy that encompasses price and wage controls. As a practicing lawyer in Chicago, I had some personal experience with federal rent controls between 1949 and 1952, when post World War II regulations were still in effect. This experience explained much to me about the operations of wage-price regulation. Many people regarded rent controls as a farce. If we have to resort to such controls, we are going to be kidding ourselves about inflation, and we are going to be in a situation where inflation is merely being camouflaged. Let me be specific. I think there were few landlords in Chicago during the period in question who were not violating the rent law. The stated rent usually was in compliance—it was $145 or $135 or whatever—but decorating repairs, maintenance, or improvements had stopped or been reduced. The rent remained the same, but it was buying much less than before. There was little the government could do about it. It would have required an enormous army of people to have monitored and policed these violations. So the first thing is that when controls come along, one way to get around them is to reduce quality or quantity. Second was that there were payments "under the table"—to obtain vacated apartments—and as far as I know, no one was ever invited from the Bureau of Labor Statistics to record the impact on the price level. And third, some landlords simply did not comply with the required rent schedule. Then there is the cost of controls, they do not come free, for government has to establish implementation and enforcement machinery. Probably the most adverse part of the whole thing is its effect on production—by cutting profit margins, price controls inhibit investment. Inhibiting production reduces supply and leads to higher prices. The country's previous experiences with price controls and other forms of economic regulation should tell us that before we abdicate these decisions to government, there always ought to be an extremely strong and compelling reason for such actions.

John Kenneth Galbraith's Rebuttal

Thank you, Mr. Chairman, you are being more than generous with me, because I used a fair amount of my previous half hour to correct Professor Siegan. He is for good regulation and against bad regulation, and I find myself coming out at about that point too. Now that he has come to concede that a substantial amount of regulation is inescapable in a modern economy, I do not feel totally unhappy.

I do want to make two points. Taking a vote of economists or studying their research on a subject is not an avenue to truth or wise policy. The economics profession has been committed for half a century to what has come to be called neoclassical economics. This envisages a society in which there are only passive and very easygoing unions, and in which monopoly is an extreme exception (the neoclassical view antedates the rise of the large corporations). Moreover, it is a world in which the market rules. When you turn these people loose to make a study of regulation, you know where they are going to come out, and that only 80 percent of them came out in favor of deregulation I think is enormously encouraging. I would remind you (since we both genuflect at the mention of the name) that Alfred Marshall said, in effect, that no economist should fear anything so much as being with the majority.

The other point involves agreement between Professor Siegan and myself. I have never been a partisan of rent control in isolation. It is a very dubious social instrument. It discriminates against a particular type of investment; it inspires precisely the type of law-breaking or evasion that he suggests. So I have no quarrel with him on that. Whenever he is right, I concede and even rejoice.

But in return, I would ask him to recognize that we do in this country have strong trade unions and other strongly organized groups, all capable of increasing their money income, and I do not think anybody in this room is going to doubt that ability. We also have strong business enterprises capable of stimulating this process and passing the cost onto the public and perhaps something more. This is not a theory; it is a condition with which we must deal. To repeat, we have three ways of dealing with it. One is to have enough unemployment so that the unions are deterred and the business firms are forced to resist union claims. Another is to accept inflation. Or we can attempt, as other countries are attempting, some form of direct stabilization effort.

It was not our experience during World War II that this was a failure. We had an enormous surplus of demand during those years and zero unemployment. In addition, we somehow or other managed to hold the line on prices for 4 long years. It was my conclusion at the end of that time (I was concerned with this for only the first 2 years) that where the large enterprises were concerned (steel, automobiles, weapons), the exercise of restraint was not all that difficult. When it was all over, I went back to Harvard and wrote, as regards industrial prices (which is where the problem of power arises), that it is not too difficult to fix prices that are already fixed.

If Professor Siegan's market still existed, we would not be talking about controls because fiscal policy and monetary policy would work. The market does not. Power has passed over to business enterprises and to trade union organizations. They can fix prices and incomes. Public controls replace private controls. That is not an easy thing to do, but it is by no means as difficult as he suggests. And, I swear, it is not as difficult as controlling rents in Mayor Daley's Chicago.

Questions and Answers

Q: Are either of you gentlemen aware of the discussions now going on nationally as well as locally here in San Diego regarding a relatively new technology in our society, cable television? A recent circuit court decision in St. Louis decided that the FCC had overstepped its grounds by mandating public access channels that we of course enjoy here in San Diego. I am wondering if either of you have any comment on this, and whether you think maybe it would contribute to local regulation, and maybe that would be more preferable. I would like your comments, if you have any, on that subject.

Siegan: I am familiar with the case, and I was very happy about it. To me, it is another instance of the courts looking at regulation and telling the FCC, "You have no basis for what you are doing." It also is consistent with an environment that I think is developing in the courts to look more critically at regulation.

Q: Would you address the second part of my question? Would you condone or would you see in a better light local regulation so we can preserve the public's right to some peace?

Siegan: No, I would not want any economic regulation at all. I want to preserve the public's right through competition. I want to make sure that you or whoever runs the cable system does the right thing. I do not want some bureau of six people deciding what you should do or what you should not do. I think you will do much better, you will serve us much better, if you compete with somebody else. Therefore, no economic regulation, locally, at the state level, or at the federal level, would be my option.

Q: In 1949 a book was published by the Yale University Press, called *Human Action* and authored by Ludwig von Mises. The *Book Review Digest* of 1949 listed several individuals who were supposed to review the book. One of them who was not sympathetic with Professor Mises' views said, "A profound work, displaying an encyclopedic mind, ought to prove thought-provoking for every reader whether he disagrees, as the reviewer, or not. Too difficult for the general public, the book is suitable for scholars only.'' But a young professor named John Kenneth Galbraith also was asked to review the book, and he stated that ''the market, despite all its virtues, does not pay for all books that deserve publication, and it is therefore both appropriate and good that a university press made this one available, but surely it should do so with some obligation to scholarly restraint.'' The question I have for Professor Galbraith, and I would like Professor Siegan to respond to it, is in light of Milton Friedman winning the Nobel Prize in economics last year and Mises' protege Hayek winning the Prize the year before, do you have any comment to make on your 1949 review of *Human Action?*

Galbraith: Oh, I could comment on that, certainly. Actually, I must defend Hayek; he and Mises were contemporaries, and he would not like to be called a protégé. I think they are both the same age; actually, Hayek may be 4 or 5 years younger. The *New York Times* sent me that book that spring and did not want the review until autumn. It was a lovely summer in Vermont, and every time I wanted to relax, there was the book staring at me. Mises—I have to tell you, this has nothing to do with ideology—published the same book over several times. So the book, among other faults, also lacked novelty. I reviewed that book by a device that I never used for any other book: I opened it at random and read one page every night. I often read the same page over again. That was such a small investment of time that the boredom did not bother me much. The books is a prodigious amount of dreary, repetitive prose or some approximation thereto. I reacted not to the printing of the book, but as a Harvard professor must to the Yale University Press plug on the jacket that said that it was the greatest intellectual exercise since Saint Thomas Aquinas. I think I should ask my colleague, who probably has a more favorable view of Mises, to say a word in his defense.

Siegan: Certainly. I think it is an excellent book. You know, I have been reading some of your books, and maybe I will be spending some time in Vermont one summer!

Q: Professor Galbraith, you talk about business restraint; you talk about labor restraint; you talk about farm restraint; you talk about various groups in our society increasing their incomes; and you also talk about the problem that for some reason there is a deep, great structural difference between society now and society 15 or 20 years ago, when being an economist was such an easy thing. You do not mention government income. Do you not think that the real difference between society today and society 15 to 20 years ago (when it was so much easier to be an economist) is the fact that government spending, say, plotted against GNP in the United States is now 35 percent, in Great Britain it is 55 to 60 percent, and the place where there has been no restraint whatever is in the government, and that Milton Friedman, whom you love to deprecate, for whatever reason, is correct in saying that it is the government and the Federal Reserve Board, in creating money to pay for the deficits of this enormous government, that really is causing the inflation and not the relationships among labor and big business and so on, that the real difference is the size and scope and tyranny of government?

Galbraith: I would not want to disagree completely with that statement. Obviously, I mentioned the growing size and importance of the nonmarket sector and the pressure that exists for public services. But I hope Professor Siegan will agree as to the importance of public services and their tendency. I am only one of the many who underestimated the extraordinary costs of running large cities, the exponential increase not only in New York but in London, Rome, and Tokyo, wherever great numbers live in close proximity. I do disagree with the odd suggestion that this is a manifestation of some tyrannical force. It has been overwhelmingly in response to a broad public pressure for the services of government. Also I would like to defend myself against the charge that I have been less active in seeking a reduction of public expenditures than Milton Friedman. The large, solid, indulgent element in the budget is, of course, the vast military expenditure. And I have argued as vehemently for getting that under control as Milton Friedman has for reducing services for the average citizen and the poor.

Siegan: Just one point, which I think brings us back to the topic. Regulation cuts production, and if you limit the amount of goods and services in existence and continue pumping the same or a greater amount of money into circulation, those dollars will have less value.

Q: How do either of you feel about price regulation only in the problem areas of the economy?

Galbraith: I am with Professor Siegan completely: where the market works, I am more than content. Where the market does not work, where it has been taken over by monopoly, by oligopoly, by large-scale industry, and the power exists to perpetuate the income-price increase, there is no alternative to intervention. And of course, while this concentration does simplify the task, it does not make it simple. However, I would not contemplate intervention across the board.

Siegan: Selective price controls create their own problems. If you really stop prices from going up in one sector, there is more money around to push them up in another. Thus, when Nixon removed food prices from controls, a larger then expected jump in the cost of food occurred. Now I cannot pin that on the fact that regulation was removed in that area and maintained in other areas, but it certainly does make sense that if you keep prices down in one place, people have more money to spend elsewhere.

Galbraith: This is a problem, Professor Siegan, in your neoclassical system where all industries are alike and everybody is competitive. However, it is not a problem if prices are already fixed by monopoly or oligopoly, by a couple of thousand large firms. Then your misallocation of resources, as would be agreed within the strict framework of a neoclassical theory, has already occurred.

Siegan: I do not see how you correct price distortions with price ceilings. All you are doing is redistorting them. The point is, if you save money in one place, you are bound to have more money around to use in another place. Selective price controls make very little sense to me, and I am not exactly an advocate of any other price controls.

Galbraith: Well let me ask you this question. Would you not agree that if you are going to avoid public control where you have private price power, then you must adopt the distinctly romantic policy of trying to restore competition in that area and break up the large corporations?

Siegan: It seems to me that we have a very substantial disagreement. I think there is great competition in our economy. I remember reading in a very illustrious work that the big steel companies and the big American automobile producers controlled prices. However, whatever controls the domestic steel and automobile producers had over prices—and I do not think they did in fact have this power—they went out the window when imports came in and provided substantial competition. I am inclined to think that we have overall a highly competitive system; we have competition between lots of things. Consider the automobile market. General Motors' production competes with domestic and foreign new cars, with used cars, and sometimes with motorcycles and bicycles. Also, there is considerable competition among industries. Today someone who wants to take a vacation may go by plane, or stay at a local hotel, or perhaps buy a new car and travel. The consumer has lots of opportunities in this society. Corporations do not control consumer expenditures.

Q: I would like you to tell us a little bit more about your program. If you should carry the day and we should start dismantling the regulatory structure, how are we going to deal with the tremendous amount of money that is tied up in these capitalized monopoly interests? You took the example of the trucking company that paid over $20 million for its trucking permit. Would you wipe it out with the stroke of a pen, so you do not need permits anymore, so that fellow's investment of $20 million has just gone down the drain. How would you deal with that?

Siegan: The problems accompanying deregulation are serious ones. There has been a lot of thought given to that, you recognize. One solution is to amortize existing investment by slowly allowing competition to come in over a period of years. It is unquestionably a problem for us when one has paid large sums on the basis of no competition, and competition comes in. Someone has even suggested that the government reimburse those who paid for licenses. Current measures for airline deregulation phase in competition over a period of years so as to minimize the hardships to existing carriers. Because problems of this nature arise, we ought to be extraordinarily careful about imposing new regulation. We now know that once we have imposed regulation, processes begin that cannot readily be terminated without injuring members of the industry. It is not that the market cannot be restored, but there is an obligation that must be considered carefully, it seems to me, where the government has said to companies, "We are going to protect you from competition" and then pulls the rug from under them.

Q: One of the main thrusts of Professor Siegan's argument, you say essentially that cooptation of various regulatory bodies results in higher prices and restricted entry. But to read a quote from one of Professor Galbraith's books, "Power is not diminished by being attributed to someone else. Almost invariably it is enhanced. . . . Nothing serves the technostructure better than to attribute unpopular or socially reprehensible action to higher authority." I would say that the firms large enough to require regulation can set their prices and exercise undue control over people, and that corruption of regulatory bodies is just used as an excuse to divert the public's attention.

Siegan: I hope you did not take me to say that there was some kind of capture; I do not believe in the "capture theory," that the companies have captured the regulatory body. So it is not a question of capture; the problem of regulation is that the regulators are not as efficient or effective as the marketplace. Where is the airline going to go? How much should it charge? Should this or another route be open to this or other carriers? It is very difficult to try and do what the regulatory bodies are attempting to do, that is, both satisfy the producer by keeping prices up and comfort the consumer by keeping prices down. I do not think the airlines have captured the CAB; it is that the CAB cannot help itself in making confused, chaotic, even ridiculous kind of rules. The second part of your question is How about these big guys, how do we know that if we get rid of regulation, they will compete? Well, one of the things that led to our new thinking about CAB is what is going on with airlines in California, PSA in particular, and two airlines in Texas. Both states engage in only light regulation. Fares are lower than under CAB control. There has been some deregulation in trucking, and prices have substantially decreased. Consider the situation in

Houston, which has virtually no land-use controls, and therefore the robber barons—and you are kind of talking in terms of the robber baron idea—should be in full control there. That certainly is not true. The consumer is doing better in Houston, where there are no controls, than anyplace else where there are controls. The notion that the big development or airline companies will monopolize production and supply is not true. I think the evidence that we have, as I have indicated, would suggest that there will be competition in the airline industry once governmental obstructionism is removed.

Q: I would like to address my question to Professor Galbraith. In your recent *New Republic* article, you referred to a situation where business and labor have control over both their incomes and the prices they set, and you also referred to this as an irresistible historical trend. I wondered why you considered this irresistible. Do you consider it to be human nature to never be satisfied, or in other words, would you say E.F. Schumacher is an incurable romanticist, and if so, why?

Galbraith: There are technological and other imperatives. If we are going to get oil down from Alaska or from under the North Sea, or if we are going to make automobiles on the present scale, we are going to have to have big firms. They are going to have to know in advance what their prices are going to be; they cannot have Professor Siegan's kind of competitive prices. If General Motors (GM) is to put $300 million or $400 million into an automobile, it must have some assurance as to what its price will be when it comes out. And GM must even control the consumer to some degree and be sure that people will want that particular combination of novelty and banality that comes out 3 years from now. In other words, the modern style of life, which I am disposed to accept as given, makes necessary the powerful business institution. And I have very little confidence in the anti-trust laws as instruments for breaking it up, for reversing the process. We have had these laws now for 90 years. In a world in which there is an overproduction of lawyers, I can understand why lawyers are in favor of them. I just do not think that they have altered the course of history appreciably. As far as E.F. Schumacher is concerned, he was an old friend, my assistant and deputy during the war. He was one of the most attractive men I have ever known, but there is no close operative connection between Schumacher's vision of a world in which things were small and nothing was large and incomprehensible and the means by which you got to that world.

Q: Possibly the size of these corporations and of the labor unions goes in hand with the law of economics that says there is unlimited wants and only so many supplies or so many resources. And I would say that Schumacher would possibly say that this could be undone by lessening your wants.

Galbraith: Perhaps he would. But here I find myself solidly on the side of Professor Siegan. Does one extend one's value system to other people? I am uncomfortable about that. Perhaps we have too many automobiles. But I am not quite prepared to tell anybody that he should not have one.

Q: This is addressed to either gentleman. Professor Galbraith seemed to imply that there was a cause-and-effect relationship between the rise of economic regulations in the 1930s and the economic recovery that took place at the end of that decade. Now there was a rise in economic regulations, we can all agree, and there was an economic recovery. Would either of you gentlement comment on whether or not it was a cause-and-effect relationship?

Galbraith: I certainly made that point. I would attribute much importance to what we have come to call the Keynesian revolution, to the notion that the state intervenes to sustain purchasing power. This had a lot to do with the relative well-being of the industrial countries in the fifties and the sixties.

Siegan: Government had a major responsibility for the woes of the 1930s. First, Milton Friedman attributes the severity of the Depression to the erroneous conduct of the Federal Reserve, which during that period instead of pushing down on the accelerator, put on the brakes and substantially limited the money supply. The money supply dropped one-third between 1929 and 1933, severely contracting the economy. The second part of my response concerns the regulatory agencies created by the New Deal. The regulation which the New Deal foisted upon us at that time had a great deterrent effect on businessmen. My conclusion, therefore, to what happened during that period of time is (1) because of the monetary policies of the Federal Reserve and (2) because of the regulatory policies then introduced, the economic decline was prolonged and more severe than it should have been. The experience should serve to caution us about government intervention.

Q: I would like to address this to both of you. With the present situation in terms of regulation—level, the degree, the kind—do you think, both of you, that a switch can be made to less, more sensible regulation without substantial economic chaos? And perhaps the steel industry would be the best example of this.

Siegan: I am a free trade man. The Federal Trade Commission (FTC) has studied the Carter administration's "reference prices" plan for the steel industry that will impose duties on foreign steel priced below a certain reference figure. The Commission study said the plan would cost consumers $1 billion annually. The FTC also made the point that parts of the steel industry were competitive with foreign production, and the President's plan would create a price shield for these steel products.

Q: My question, though, is what is the effect of this, of deregulation of the steel industry, whether you did it across the board all at once or by degrees?

Siegan: You do not mean deregulation of the steel industry; we have been talking about deregulation of an industry that is already regulated, such as airlines or trucking?

Q: I guess I was not quite clear, but when I speak of regulation of, say, the steel industry, I am talking about price supports, duties, import quotas, things like this, antidumping regulations. Like you say, they, in effect, shield the steel industry from outright competition from foreign sources. We can apply this in other industries also in differing degrees and with differing regulations, but my basic question is, would outright deregulation of all these various facets of our economy bring about substantial chaos?

Siegan: Let us look at those industries which are regulated. I think the best thing that could happen for the airline industry is to deregulate it. We will get more companies; we will cut fares; we will be able to get the kind of benefits for the consumer that Laker has shown us are obtainable. Laker has given an economics lesson to the airline industry (and he does not even come from the University of Chicago). His lesson is that by cutting fares, you can attract a lot of traffic. Laker is doing well, and other airlines are now following his lead and are not suffering. For a long time the airlines were not concentrating enough on competition. When regulation comes around, the airline thinks of how to beat the regulator and the regulations. It is more important to get CAB approval than it is to get passenger approval. When there is regulation, the regulator can do an awful lot for you. He can give you new routes; he can cut competition on routes—do all kinds of things. So what has been happening in the airline industry is that the big companies have been motivated more toward doing something about CAB regulations than doing anything about competition. Well, they have been forced by the Laker situation, by the threat of CAB deregulation, to think in terms of competition. I think that is the healthiest thing that could happen. As more deregulation occurs, I think we will get more people in the airline industry with bigger and better ideas.

Insofar as import quotas are concerned, there is always an enormous tradeoff. There is the question of steel workers that are going to be unemployed if duties or quotas are not imposed. On the other hand, the FTC points out that consumers will be paying $1 billion annually if such regulations are created. I think history tells us that it is better to stick with free rather than regulated trade. It is certainly not an easy question for the people in Youngstown who are going to lose work in the absence of steel tariffs. But I think history shows us that free trade is wise in the short term and clearly desirable in the long term.

Q.   My question is directed mostly to Professor Siegan, but also to Professor Galbraith if he cares to comment. We have been talking quite a bit tonight about the demand for government services and also the effect of government spending on inflation and what have you. Recently Milton Friedman came out in support of what we have here in California known as the "Jarvis amendment." He thought it was a good way to start cutting down on government expenditures, and we do have talk that school districts will cut their staffs by 50 percent. Even the County Planning Department is thinking of cutting back 50 percent, which might get us away from the zoning Professor Siegan's not in favor of. There are two things about the Jarvis amendment. One would prefer to see government services cut back like this or, philosophically, should the state pick up the tab? Do you think it would be good philosophically to have the property tax burden shift to the income tax or the sales tax?

Galbraith: No, I would not. When a companion measure was up 4 or 5 years ago, I had a debate with the then governor, my old distinguished ADA colleague, Ronald Reagan, on the subject. I do not think this is a good manifestation of democratic process, and I must say I go back to a point that I made *ad nauseam,* which certainly could group me with Ludwig von Mises for repetition. There is nothing inherently inferior about public services. I have never been able to understand why clean houses and dirty streets were a sort of ultimate expression of civilization in New York, or that schools were somehow inferior to television. It seems to me that public services are not intrinsically less needed or less useful than private goods.

Siegan: May I answer that question in principle, without getting into the Jarvis–Gann situation? I think the only way you can stop spending is to put a lid on it, a constitutional lid. In principle, I very much advocate a lid on the spending process. The point, I think, that has to be made is that currently there is almost reckless abandon at the local and state levels on spending. Enormous political pressure exists for ever increased spending, and I do not think it is possible for the political apparatus to counter it. The political process simply is not set up to say "no" to a lot of people who say "spend a little bit more."

Notes

1. Quoted in Michael McMenamin, "The Curious Politics of Deregulation," *Reason,* January 1978, p. 24

2. Ralph Nader, "Statement on Regulatory Reforms to the Consumer and Environmental Subcommittees," U.S. Senate Committee on Commerce, June 23, 1975, p. 2.

3. McMenamin, "The Curious Politics," p. 27.

4. Virginia State Board of Pharmacy v. Virginia Citizens Consumer Council, Inc., 425 U.S. 748 (1976).

5. Linmark Associates, Inc. v. Township of Willingboro, 437 U.S. 85 (1977).

6. Bates v. State Bar of Arizona, 433 U.S. 350 (1977).

7. Carey v. Population Servs. Int'l., 431 U.S. 678 (1977).

8. Milton Kafaglis, "A Paradox of Regulated Trucking," *Regulation,* Sept.–Oct. 1977, p. 27.

9. Thomas Gale Moore, "The Beneficiaries of Trucking Regulation," *Journal of Law and Economics* 21, (1978): 327.

10. Bernard H. Siegan, *Land Use Without Zoning* (Lexington, Mass.: LexingtonBooks, D.C. Heath and Co., 1972).

11. Lee Benham, "The Effect of Advertising on the Price of Eyeglasses," *Journal of Law and Economics* 15 (1972): 337.

12. Mason Gaffney, "Containment Policies for Urban Sprawl," in *Approaches to the Study of Urbanization,* Richard Stauber, ed., p. 124. (Lawrence, Ka.: Univ. of Kansas, 1964).

13. *The MacNeil/Lehrer Report,* a coproduction of WNET/13, New York, and WETA/26, Washington, D.C., January 10, 1978.

2

Should the Minimum Wage Law Be Abolished?

Walter E. Williams and
Stephen J. Solarz

Walter Williams's Presentation

In this discussion, we must focus on a point that does not often enter consideration of many issues that we face today: What are the effects of the rules of the game on various outcomes of that game? For example (to give you an intuitive feel for the significance of the rules of the game on the outcomes), I would state (and you would probably agree with me) that you could not find five females throughout the world who could compete with the Los Angeles Lakers in a basketball game. One might ask the question, "Why is it that women cannot beat the Los Angeles Lakers at playing basketball?" Some people would say that women are shorter than men or that women are not as fast as men or that men have more muscle mass and muscle power than women, but all these answers would be wrong.

The reason that you cannot find five women who, as a team, could beat the Los Angeles Lakers is the rules of the game. If you told the commissioner of basketball to rewrite the rules of the game so that women would win, the task could easily be done. These rules would require, for example, that the game be played in high-heeled shoes or that an intricate doily be knitted before a fast break could be made, or something very similar. The point that I am trying to make is that rule changes affect outcomes. As the rules are written now, they weigh the game in favor of those who are tall and fast and have a lot of muscle power. If you rewrite the rules, you can weigh the game in favor of those who have less speed. So keep this in mind as we address the issue of the minimum wage law, for in our society this law is one of the rules of the game of employment.

I share the value that most Americans share—that all people should have the highest standard of living obtainable. Is the minimum wage consistent with this value? Minimum wage legislation affects the right of free individuals to enter into those contracts which they (not us, but they) perceive as being remunerative within their set of choices. It is quite clear to all of us (contrary perhaps to the United States Constitution) that we are not all made equal by our Maker. By accident of birth, some of us have physical attributes that are highly valued by the market, such as reflexes and high powers of tonal discrimination. These characteristics give some of us superior talents as tennis players, instrumentalists, or basketball players. On the other hand, many of us find ourselves members of minority groups treated unfairly in the past and in the present. As a consequence, upward mobility from poverty is a doubly difficult task. Many people are born under conditions in which poverty is an everyday fact of life, unemployment is the natural state of affairs, and the meager resources for life's sustenance come from handouts.

One of the most important policy considerations that confronts today's society is how to help the less fortunate to become independent, enterprising, and upwardly mobile? No one here (or in the whole country for that matter) knows the answer to this question. This fact is evidenced by the failure of much legislation, thousands of cases of civil rights litigation, and billions of tax dollars to produce a solution to the problem. However, it is clear that we cannot help the less fortunate by harming them. While this statement may be viewed as unnecessary, it is a proposition that is often ignored in the discussion and formulation of policy. People assume that just because a policy *intends* to help the disadvantaged, the policy will in fact produce the desired effect. We have to recognize that good intentions alone may produce the opposite result. There may be no relationship between good intentions and good results.

The Fair Labor Standards Act of 1938 is one of those good intentions. It provided for a minimum wage of 25 cents per hour, which was periodically increased to $2.65 an hour in January 1979, and which will eventually go up to $3.50 an hour in 1981. Defenders of minimum wage legislation say that this legislation protects low-income workers from substandard wages and exploitation. It is also argued that in preventing low wages, the minimum wage law acts as an antipoverty weapon.

Many of the moral issues that have surrounded the minimum wage law debates, such as substandard wages, worker exploitation, and the like, are quite difficult to evaluate, for with moral issues it is impossible to formulate testable hypotheses. But what we can do is ask cause-and-effect questions and find answers to what is the effect of raising the minimum wage. One important effect rests on an important limitation of congressional powers; Congress cannot do everything. It is clear that legislative bodies have the power to legislate wage increases. Unfortunately, legislative bodies do not have the corresponding power to legislate increases in worker productivity. Secondly, although Congress may legislate the price at which a labor transaction may occur, it has not chosen to legislate that the transaction actually occur. Thus Congress may tell employers that if they hire people, they must pay them a minimum of $2.65 an hour, but it has not chosen to tell employers that they *must* hire people.

To the extent that the minimum wage law raises the pay level above the productivity of some workers, employers will predictably make adjustments in the usage of labor. On the one hand, such adjustments benefit some workers—namely, those who get jobs and receive higher wages. The adverse effects of the minimum wage law, however, will be felt by those workers who lose their jobs or fail to get jobs in the first place. These workers are the most marginal in the labor force. For example, if an employer has to pay a worker $2.65 an hour, he has very little incentive to hire a worker whose output value is $1.50 an hour. He has incentive to hire only those workers who can produce $2.65 worth of goods and services per hour. Thus, the minimum wage law discriminates against the unskilled worker.

The distributional impact of legislated minimums is an interesting issue. As I have said, the worker who bears the heaviest burden of the minimum wage law is the worker who has the lowest skills or the worker who is viewed by employers as very costly to hire. In the U.S. labor force, two very well identified subgroups have those characteristics. One is youths, who, because of their age and lack of experience, have few skills. The second subgroup (which contains members of the first) consists of racial minorities (such as blacks and Hispanics), who, as a result of discrimination and other socioeconomic factors, are disproportionately represented among low-skilled people. Not only are these workers made unemployable by the minimum wage law, but they also are severely limited in their opportunities to upgrade their skills by on-the-job training.

It is no accident that these groups who have the lowest skills are the most highly represented among the unemployment statistics. Minority youth unemployment ranges from three to seven times that of the general labor force. Nationally, black youth unemployment has ranged from two to three times that for white youths. In some metropolitan areas, such as Oakland, California, the unemployment rate among black youths is 70 percent. Although many people are familiar with the most recent statistics on youth unemployment, not many are aware of the black-white unemployment statistics for earlier periods of our country. For example, in 1948, black youth unemployment was roughly the same as white youth unemployment. During that year, blacks aged sixteen to seventeen had an unemployment rate *less* than whites of comparable age; black youths had a 9.4 percent unemployment rate compared with a 10.2 percent rate for whites. From that period up until the early 1950s, black youths were more active in the labor market than were white youths. The participation rates of black youths was 108 percent of white youths. At present, that participation rate is 50 percent of that for white youths, and the rate is falling.

Faced with these statistical facts, one naturally asks the question. "Why have labor market opportunities dropped so precipitously for black youths?" Can racial discrimination explain this kind of reversal? Can we say that in 1948 American society was less racially discriminatory than it is now? I do not think that we can. Can we then say that blacks in 1948 were more skilled than white youths in 1948? Again the answer is no. Nearly all academic economists who work outside government and who have studied the subject say that the minimum wage law is the single most important variable explaining the high rate of youth, black, and other minority unemployment. The racial effect of the law would exist even in the absence of racial preferences on behalf of employers. However, if all factors, such as worker productivity, remain constant, minimum wage laws provide an incentive to engage in racial discrimination. For example, in economic theory an inverse relationship exists between price and demand. The lower the price of something is, the more people take of it. Thus if you make a law requiring that all workers be paid the same wage no matter whom you hire, employers tend to hire the workers whom they like the most.

An example of this result is South African business. In South Africa, black skilled laborers in construction earn 39 cents an hour, while white skilled workers doing the same job earn $1.91 an hour. South Africa has laws reserving certain jobs for whites. But given the wage differential, contractors had an incentive to violate that law and hire blacks. The white labor unions of South Africa discovered that they were losing jobs. So they said, "Since job reservation laws no longer protect the jobs of white workers, what we need is an equal-pay-for-equal-work law (the equivalent of a minimum wage law) requiring that firms give blacks the same wages they give whites." Firms then had a greater incentive to discriminate against blacks, for it no longer cost them anything to discriminate. However, if the wage differential were 39 cents as opposed to $1.91, it would cost them $1.52 an hour to indulge their racial preferences. White unions made it explicit that they were not helping blacks, but that they were protecting their jobs by pricing blacks out of the market.

With the known adverse impact of the minimum wage laws, you might ask why we have an increasing minimum wage law in the United States. Well, who are the major lobbyists for that law? They are, of course, the labor unions. You might then ask, "Why do labor unions lobby for minimum wage laws when their members make three and four times the minimum wage?" Is the reason that they care for their downtrodden fellows? One begins to see why unions lobby for the minimum wage law when one recognizes that in some activities unskilled labor is a substitute for highly skilled labor. To get a feel for this, let us imagine that you can build a fence with either *one* highly skilled worker who gets paid $38 a day or *three* lowly skilled workers who get paid $13 a day each. With either technique, you can build the fence. Naturally, the firm, if it wanted to minimize costs, would use the one highly skilled worker because then the fence would cost only $38 as opposed to $39 (the price of the three lowly skilled workers). Now how can the highly skilled worker improve his wage? He can advocate, in the name of living wages and worker exploitation, a minimum wage law in the fencing industry of $20 a day. After that law is enacted, the highly skilled worker can go to the employer and demand a wage of $59 a day, whereas, before the enactment of the minimum wage law, had he demanded a $59-a-day salary, he would have lost his job.

Do the unions mean to do this? I do not know. Yet one has to separate the intent of one's behavior from the effects of that behavior. Sometimes intents have very little to do with effects. For example, if a truck runs me down and the driver comes to me and says, "Walter, I didn't mean to run you over," I am just as flat as if he meant to run me over. So I do not care about his intentions. Intentions become important only when we decide what kind of sentence we give the fellow. Labor unions, by advocating minimum wage and other laws that price their competition out of the market and cause unemployment among disadvantaged people, will not make their strategy viable.

We would have politically unstable situations in the United States if unemployment meant starvation. Thus, as part of the strategy to improve their wealth, labor unions also have an incentive to advocate and lobby for income maintenance, food stamps, and other such welfare programs. The effect of these programs is to cast a few crumbs to the people who are disemployed as a result of the union market activity in order to keep them quiet. Hence their labor market activity is disguised. Society pays for this outcome in two ways: as a result of people being unemployed, we pay higher taxes to support welfare programs, and as a result of higher wages, we pay higher product prices.

The fact that young people cannot get jobs would not be important if a job meant only a spending change. However, early work experiences are important to young people. Such experiences provide both training and an opportunity to acquire characteristics that will enhance their future careers. They teach young people that they must be prompt, that they must not spit in the foreman's face, and that they must come to work on Saturday even though they got paid on Friday. They provide a sense of maturity—that is, the young person comes home with his first paycheck, and he feels the pride that comes from being financially independent. Furthermore, the absence of early work opportunities spells disaster for young people (particularly minorities) in other ways. A number of studies have shown a significant relationship between the absence of work experience for youths and juvenile delinquency. To the extent that the minimum wage law contributes to unemployment among youths, it indirectly contributes to a high rate of juvenile delinquency, particularly in black communities. Another of the law's effects is to make economic development in the black communities impossible; the neighborhood cannot develop economically if it has a high crime rate.

The fact that labor unions engage in market activities that adversely affect minorities does not cause me to be antilabor or labor unions to be antiminority. Nevertheless, the effect of union activity is often antiminority. In fact, past black leaders almost unanimously condemned labor unions. Booker T. Washington was a lifelong foe of unions, and W.E.B. DuBois called them "the greatest enemy of black working people."

Other restrictions, in addition to the minimum wage law, make it difficult for young people to find employment. Many concern the work laws that are associated with the Fair Labor Standards Act. For example, one may not hire youths to work in the so-called dangerous activities. Although at some time in our history these work laws might have had a place in that they protected young people from working in mines and losing limbs, these same laws prevent today's youths from working in air-conditioned, plush offices.

The Davis-Bacon Act, another minimum wage law, also has a disemployment effect, particularly on minorities. This act is an example of the super minimum wage law that requires that workers be paid the prevailing wage on all federal construction projects. The Secretary of Labor interprets the prevailing wage as being the union wage, and the Davis-Bacon Act requires extremely high apprenticeship rates. Thus the act discriminates against nonunion contractors and nonunion workers. Statistical studies show that only 35 percent of minority construction workers reported union membership. To the extent that the Davis-Bacon Act discriminates against nonunion workers, it has a racial effect of discriminating against minorities. This racial impact was anticipated by the act's designers. During House debates, allusions to racial bigotry were made. Congressman Allgood was quite specific (and you may look this up if you wish in the records for the 71st Congress, 3d Session, 1931, p. 6513) when he said that a contractor has "cheap colored labor" that competes with white labor throughout the country. Although today's unions may not have the same kind of intent, the effect remains racially discriminatory.

In addition to minimum wage laws, I consider labor restrictions and licensing as artificial barriers to entry. The basic point is that many laws create an advantage for the more preferred people and make it almost impossible for today's disadvantaged minorities to enter the mainstream of employment *en mass* as earlier disadvantaged minorities have done. In this country, other minorities have been as despised as blacks. For example, in California, alien land laws prohibited Orientals from owning land in the United States. Yet these despised minorities (such as Japanese-Americans) have entered the mainstream *en mass*. As a matter of fact, by any measure of ethnic success, Japanese-Americans lead any group in terms of education, family stability, and so forth.

Many laws, although well-intentioned, spell disaster for large segments of the black and Hispanic communities. The most tragic element of this effect is that society will come to view the difficulty that these groups have in entering the mainstream of American society (in spite of the billions of dollars spent and the many laws enacted and the thousands of cases of civil litigation) as group incompetence. The most racist elements of our society will have their prophesies realized. Hardly anyone acknowledges that many problems encountered by these groups are due neither to group incompetence nor to individual incompetence, rather they are due to the force of government influences by powerful interest groups. Groups seeking to pursue their own objectives contribute to the enactment of laws that spell disaster for disadvantaged Americans.

Stephen Solarz's Presentation

I had an experience recently that, I think, constitutes a decisive refutation of Professor Williams's arguments. I arrived in San Diego on a cross-continental flight from Washington, and because my driver did not appear to pick me up, I had to take a cab to my destination, the University of San Diego. The cab driver had no idea where the university was located. Although he attempted to follow the dispatcher's directions, he ended up getting lost on a dirt road several miles from campus. Finally, after many mishaps we managed to locate the university. When I requested that he ask someone where the law school was, he refused on the grounds that finding the correct building was my responsibility, not his. Whereupon I told him that if that was his attitude, I would indeed get out, but that I had no intention of paying him. True to my word, I left the cab, and he did not get paid. The conclusion I draw from this story is that even without a minimum wage some people are so incompetent (this cab driver was young) that they should not be able to get a job.

It never dawned on me before Professor Williams's presentation that I might be considered an enemy of blacks or young people or other minorities because of my support for the minimum wage; therefore, I would like to reassure those of you who share my instinctive ideological commitment to a minimum wage. I am not an enemy of these groups. The way I would like to demonstrate this point is first to make the case for why the minimum wage makes sense in terms of both equity and economics and then deal with the arguments set forth by Professor Williams and others that it causes unemployment and also contributes significantly to inflation.

Historically, minimum wage laws are a product of the reaction to the sweatshop conditions under which vast numbers were forced to toil during the years when our economic system was based on the principle of undiluted and unrestrained laissez-faire capitalism. It was not uncommon in those days for someone to toil full time and still not make enough in wages to sustain himself or his family. As a result, wives and children, at the age of eight and younger, were forced into the labor markets just to provide themselves with enough food to keep from starving. A moral revulsion caused by these exploitative conditions led to calls for governmental protection for these workers, who had no bargaining power of their own. As distant as those days may now seem, the fear of returning to those brutal and primitive conditions remains a major reason for the maintenance and extention of the minimum wage and other fair labor legislation. In fact, I think that it is fair to say that the two main reasons motivating members of Congress to vote for minimum wage increases are first, a desire to protect the weakest workers in our society from exploitation and second, a feeling that individuals who work full time should, in fairness and justice, be able to acquire from their earnings the basic necessities of life.

Despite these ethical concerns and moral roots of minimum wage legislation, I do not want to give the impression that these laws are seen by members of Congress simply as acts of charity. The minimum wage has been set at an exceedingly modest level. The recently enacted minimum wage floor of $2.65 provides a full-time worker with an annual income of approximately $5,500 a year, which is $338 below the federally defined poverty level. In addition, low-wage workers are not the only beneficiaries of the minimum wage laws. Our entire society (every man and women in this room) benefits by the increased purchasing power created by raising the salaries of our lowest paid workers.

With all the recent talk about minimum wage laws causing unemployment, it is easy to forget that the first federal minimum wage law was passed during the Great Depression as part of an economic package designed to stimulate employment. The Fair Labor Standards Act, which contains the minimum wage provision, was passed 40 years ago as part of President Roosevelt's New Deal program, which also included unemployment insurance, agricultural price supports, Social Security, and federal work projects. These programs were not based on some saintly notion of social justice. The New Deal and its minimum wage component were acts of economic necessity designed to increase the purchasing power of the nation. These provisions turned penniless old people, farmers, and workers into active consumers. Indeed, the buying power of these previous nonbuyers became the cornerstone for the revival of our dormant economy. It is in large part due to these programs that we have avoided, despite all the ups and downs of our economy, a repeat of the Great Depression of the 1930s.

To briefly summarize, the argument for the minimum wage is twofold. First, the exploitative sweatshop conditions under which many workers had to toil for the first third of this century makes clear that federal intervention is needed to ensure that millions of Americans will not be working at or below subsistence levels. Second, our economic history of boom and bust before the Great Depression makes clear that federal intervention is needed to ensure that enough purchasing power exists to maintain the stable markets that are necessary for our economic well-being. The minimum wage, by placing a floor under which the earnings of working Americans cannot fall, helps maintain and stabilize markets that are necessary for our economic well-being. The argument I have just made for the minimum wage would, I think, go unchallenged by all but a very few. The goals of social justice and economic stability are hard to argue against. And the case that the minimum wage contributes substantially to these goals is clear and compelling.

Instead of attacking the minimum wage directly, however, most of its opponents have concentrated on its negative side effects, contending that minimum wage laws create both inflation and unemployment. It is to a refutation of these contentions that I would like to turn. Opponents of minimum wage laws have long claimed that increases in this bottom level of compensation are inflationary. However, the history of price increases since World War II indicates that far from being a cause of inflation, increases in the minimum wage have been a product of inflation. Let me detail the relevant data. In 1949 the minimum wage was increased by 87.5 percent from 40 cents an hour to 70 cents an hour. The inflation rate the following year was 1 percent. In 1956 the minimum wage was increased by 33⅓ percent. During the year following that increase the inflation rate increased by 1.5 percent. In 1961 the minimum wage was increased by 15 cents to $1.15 an hour. During the year following that increase the inflation rate was approximately 1 percent. In 1963 the minimum wage was raised to $1.25 per hour. The inflation rate for the year following that increase was 1.3 percent. The minimum wage was again raised in annual increments in both 1967 and 1968 to a level of $1.60 an hour. The inflation rate for the first 6 months following these increases was 1.1 and 1.9 percent, respectively. As can be seen from these figures, the minimum wage had had either a negligible effect or no effect at all on the rate of inflation.

However, our recent history demonstrates that rampant inflation is clearly the primary cause for increases in the minimum wage. Although I was not a member of Congress during the enactment of the legislation that brought the minimum wage up from $1.60 to $2.30 an hour, I have no doubt that the last two minimum wage bills were passed in order to counter the erosion of purchasing power that inflation had caused in the budgets of low-wage workers. In fact, if one takes a look at the real purchasing power of the minimum wage, one finds that it has actually declined since 1968, when the minimum wage stood at $1.60 in current dollars. (Using 1961 as the base year, the real minimum wage in 1968 was $1.41.)

In April 1974 the value of the $1.60 minimum wage had plummeted in real terms to $1. The increases enacted by the Ninety-Third Congress in early 1974 raised the real value of the minimum wage only slightly over $1.20 an hour, or 20 cents less than it was in 1968. Moreover, the current increase to $2.65 an hour is also nothing more than an attempt to keep pace with inflation. Indeed, the real value of the latest increase will be only $1.27 an hour, still substantially lower than the value of the $1.60 minimum wage in 1968.

Although I am not an economist, I would like to venture an explanation for why increases in the minimum wage do not have much impact on the inflation rate. The fact is that the people who directly benefit from an increase in the minimum wage constitute a small percentage of the entire work force and the increase in their pay caused by a rise in the minimum wage constitutes an even smaller percentage of the nation's labor costs. For example, the current increase in the minimum wage will affect the wages only of those Americans who earn between $2.30 and $2.65 an hour. Such workers number only 4.5 million and constitute only 4.9 percent of the current work force. Increases in their wages will amount only to $2.2 billion per year, or less than two-tenths of 1 percent of our total wage bill. Other factors also mitigate the effects of increases in the minimum wage on the price levels for the country as a whole. Some studies have indicated that firms that are affected by minimum wage laws are exploitative and wasteful of their labor. When they are mandated to increase their wages, they pay their workers; they do not risk losing their markets by raising their prices inordinately. Instead, they lower their profit margins, tighten up their management, or use their employees more efficiently.

Not content to raise the false flag of inflation, however, opponents of the minimum wage also raise the tattered banner of unemployment. The argument that increases in the minimum wage will lead to unemployment is not, of course, a new one. Opponents of wage floors have used that tattered argument and fear of layoffs for as long as the Congress has been considering the minimum wage law (at least 40 years). As a matter of fact, opponents of the enactment of the first minimum wage claimed that the establishment of a 25 cent an hour minimum wage in 1938 would force the wholesale firing of millions of workers, whose productivity (they claimed) would not justify a salary of 25 cents an hour.

The argument that a wage minimum would hurt the employment opportunities of unskilled workers was used in the effort to have a lower minimum applied to the South, where opponents of the minimum wage claimed labor was less productive. Although the movement to have a regional differential in the minimum wage failed, the fear of unemployment among less-skilled workers did exclude agricultural workers from the coverage of the minimum wage laws until the 1970s. The phenomenal growth of nonagricultural employment in the South since 1938, when the minimum wage went into effect, and the corresponding decline in farm employment during the same period puts the lie to the theory that increases in the wages of those at the bottom of the wage ladder will lead to their firing.

In addition to these macro and global kinds of trends, more specific instances exist to refute the argument that increases in the minimum wage result in unemployment. Much of their evidence comes from official government documents. The Fair Labor Standards Act, for example, requires the Secretary of Labor to make annual reports to Congress and to the President on the specific impact of the minimum wage on unemployment.

None of the numerous reports that have been filed pursuant to that legislation indicate that any increase in unemployment levels was due to a rise in the minimum wage. I am sure that some skeptics might attribute the results of these reports to a desire by the various Secretaries of Labor to justify either their policy recommendations or their ideological convictions. However, such a theory would not explain the reports to this effect made early in the Nixon administration by Secretary of Labor Schultz. The Nixon administration took office soon after increases in the minimum wage made during the Johnson administration became effective. Because President Nixon was opposed to any increases in the minimum wage during his entire first term of office, and because the new administration had a stake in discrediting the economic policies of the old administration, the conditions seemed ripe for a report that would detail the negative effect of the recent increase, if in fact there was any. Yet despite the politics of the situation, the 1970 report of the Secretary of Labor (a report that was wholly controlled by Nixon appointees) found that employment continued to rise during the period of the minimum wage increases and that in the region where the minimum wage had its greatest impact "employment rose substantially." There was nothing in Secretary Schultz's report linking the minimum wage to unemployment, even though the politics of the situation called for precisely such a conclusion. It is safe, therefore, to conclude that the reason that no relationship was reported was that none exists.

The reason that some economists have claimed that there is a cause-and-effect relationship between an increase in the minimum wage and rises in umemployment is that their analysis is both incomplete and based on some unproven assumptions. Their analysis is incomplete in that it views employees simply as a production cost and not as potential consumers. However, workers are both producers and consumers. When their wages increase, so does their purchasing power and so does the market for goods in the areas in which they reside. Thus although the minimum wage may force employers to pay more for workers to produce their product, it also expands the markets for their products by increasing their workers' purchasing power. It is therefore no coincidence that markets and products have expanded most significantly in the South, where the impact of the minimum wage has been the greatest.

Opponents of the minimum wage are also wrong because the theory on which they base their analysis has little relationship to reality. They have long maintained that wages are set by the marginal productivity of each worker and that pay rates are determined by the additional amounts each worker produces. Under this theory, if wage rates are increased by nonmarket forces (such as the minimum wage), the workers' salaries will exceed the value of their production, and employers will find it profitable to lay off large sections of their work force.

Although this theory is logically consistent, it bears no resemblance to the actual way that firms set their wage rates. For example, even if firms wanted to set salaries based on the marginal productivity of their labor, they could not do so; there is simply no way to determine the value of the labor of an individual employee working in a service industry or an integrated manufacturing process. No employer can determine the amount produced by an additional janitor or another person on the assembly line. It simply cannot be done; therefore, there is no way that the salaries of these people can be determined in such a fashion. Even if the marginal productivity of workers could be ascertained, wages would not be determined by that calculation. Instead, wages would be set as they are now, by the replacement cost of labor. No employer will pay $3 an hour to an employee who is producing $4 worth of goods if the employer finds someone who will work for $2 an hour and produce the same amount. After all, no income-producing institution would limit itself to a $1 profit when it could easily be making a $2 profit. And in a high-unemployment, loose-labor market, there are always workers who are willing to work for very little. As a result, competition among low-skilled workers depresses their wage rates far below anything resembling their true value. If one applies the model I have just drawn to the U.S. economy during the last half century, one finds that with the exception of a very brief period during World War II, a substantial surplus of unskilled labor has existed in the United States, and that the model describes the U.S. very well.

As a result, there is always a reserve army of unemployed workers who will work for extremely low wages and from which employers may choose. This situation existed especially in the small towns of the South and West, where one or two employers can dominate the labor market and where the political climate does not allow union organizing that can equalize the bargaining power between employers and employees. Given the economic reality, the minimum wage does not create any disincentives for employment. In these situations, the minimum wage acts only as a restraint on the exploitative conditions that otherwise would exist because of the unequal bargaining power between employers and unskilled, unorganized employees.

Finally, I want to qualify something I said before. Although the evidence is clear that increases in the minimum have no, or little, negative effect on the overall employment level in the country, there are undoubtedly a few individuals whose skills are so poor that they are priced out of the market by an increase in the minimum. However, common sense requires the broad promulgation of rules to be geared to the dominant conditions in the society and not to a few aberrations. It would, therefore, be unwise, as Dr. Williams advocates, to repeal a statute that protects millions of employees so that a relatively small number of unskilled individuals can be given the opportunity to work at wage levels that may be below subsistence and that will undoubtedly be inadequate for maintaining a decent life in this society. Although the requirements of public policy must be geared to meet the needs of the overwhelming majority, the needs of the minority, however minuscule, should not be neglected. Thus I, like many other congressmen, voted to increase the minimum wage, but I have also been in favor of and voted for establishing large-scale training programs that will improve the skill levels of those who might be adversely affected by the minimum wage.

I think it is both interesting and ironic that the very people who oppose an increase in the minimum wage on the grounds that it will hurt the minorities and the poor are the ones who also tend to oppose the establishment of government programs designed to generate jobs for the poor and the blacks. To me this position seems strikingly inconsistent.

Walter Williams's Rebuttal

Congressman Solarz says that the minimum wage law is meeting the needs of the majority. He is quite right about that. The minimum wage law meets the needs of the majority because teenagers and minorities are in the minority, and the minimum wage law works against their interests. When economists argue that the minimum wage law has an adverse effect on employment, they are not saying that it reduces total employment, but that it has an adverse effect on the most disadvantaged segments of the labor market. Indeed, labor market statistics show that minority youth unemployment has risen from 9.2 percent in 1948 to well over 40 percent today. Now if the minimum wage law had the beneficial effects that its proponents give it, such as being an antipoverty tool and making workers better off, would we not have a wonderful policy for helping underdeveloped countries? All we would need to do is go over and tell the leaders of these countries that they need a minimum wage law high enough that their workers can have a decent wage. But minimum wage laws do not have that magical problem-solving effect.

Congressman Solarz mentioned the comments of Secretary Schultz, but he failed to mention those of the present Secretary of Labor, Ray Marshall, who said that the effects of the minimum wage law will be to reduce employment by 90,000 people. He has also said, as did Congressman Solarz, that we have programs such as CETA that will hire more teenagers; however, we are funding these at 80,000 jobs. So there is already a net loss without entering into the very, very large existing pool.

Congressman Solarz suggested that economists did not know what they were talking about with respect to the unemployment effects of the initial minimum wage of 25 cents on the growth rates during World War II. Now one has to realize that the real wage is the determinant of the amount of labor to be hired. The minimum wage of 25 cents an hour was first enacted in 1938 and was not amended for quite a while. Inflation effectively repealed the minimum wage law by increasing so rapidly during that period that 25 cents amounted to nothing. Of course, it would not have the adverse effects on employment. But when we started amending the minimum wage law regularly, it began to have some of the effects that we have talked about.

I am worried about one other aspect of the unemployment problem of minorities and low-skilled people in our major metropolitan areas. Many politicians advocate governmental programs as a solution to the unemployment problem. What this approach suggests is the creation of various programs such as leaf-raking, washing graffiti off walls, and mending fences in Arizona—programs that do not prepare people very well for work in the private sector. These programs will make minorities a permanent welfare class, permanently dependent on the government. Allowing the socioeconomic welfare of minorities to depend on the particular administration in power is a very poor strategy for any policymaker, because administrations and Congresses come and go. I surely do not want to make the socioeconomic development of blacks dependent on that.

When the youth differential came up as a recent amendment to the minimum wage law, the vote was tied, and "Tip" O'Neill "tipped" the vote, so to speak, against the youth differential. The arguments that Congressman Solarz and others bring up show a kind of schizophrenia. On the one hand, they say that the minimum wage law does not very significantly affect youth unemployment, but on the other hand, they will vote down the youth differential because they all say, "If you lower the minimum wage, more sons will get jobs, and their fathers will be unemployed." Now which is it? Does the minimum wage law have an effect, or does it not? The whole father and son notion assumes that there is a finite number of jobs available in this society; if one person gets employed, then of necessity someone else has to be unemployed. Our labor market was less than 1 million in 1776, and now it is 94 million, showing no evidence of a finite number of jobs over that period. If we had the youth differential, hotels would be willing to hire more people to keep the hallways cleaner, and more supermarkets would hire bag boys at the checkout stands. There would be a net gain in employment. Of course, there would be some substitution; some firms would fire a man if they could hire a boy cheaper. But on the whole, there would be an increase in employment and a fall in the general level of prices.

One thing forgotten in much of this debate is that higher wages do not necessarily bring higher purchasing power. Americans have been receiving higher wages for a long time, and a lot of the purchsing power has been eroded. If I earned 20 cents an hour in wages and potatoes were a dime a pound, my real wage would be 2 pounds of potatoes. This would not change if I made a dime an hour and potatoes were a nickel a pound. It has been said that the ratio of the minimum wage to the manufacturing wage has not changed that much, but what has happened is that there has been a shifting in the productivity level at which firms are willing to hire employees. That is, the higher general level of wages forces firms to seek the most qualified individuals. This is a part of the minimum wage law that is being ignored.

I do not believe that the minimum wage law is a very significant cause of inflation, inflation being defined as a general rise in the price level. Inflation can come about only by an increase in the money supply. The U.S. government, through its transactions in the money market increasing the money supply, creates inflation.

You cannot rewrite any law without having some losers and some beneficiaries. In the case of abolishing the minimum wage law, you would reduce the monopoly of powers of those who gain from the minimum wage law. I cannot say that society would be better off if the minimum wage law were abolished, because that would require a value judgment on my behalf, but the point is clear that young and disadvantaged people are made worse off by the minimum wage law. Teenagers have no representation in Congress. Since they do not vote, they have no political power. And if you are going to hurt someone, you might as well hurt those people without any political power, those who cannot hurt you back. Thus we have decided that we are going to have a set of game rules that will be at the expense of teenagers.

One has to recognize that the only way the less preferred people can compete with more preferred people—higher skilled, for example—is to offer what we call in economics a compensating difference. Through the minimum wage law, teenagers have been denied the opportunity to offer a compensating difference, which in their case means bidding down their prices so that the employer will hire them.

I oppose the various make-work programs endorsed by Congressman Solarz. Programs such as CETA have a substitution effect: they do not reach the targeted group, and they have to be financed. The government does not sit on top of Mount Olympus with all this wealth; it is the private citizen who must reduce the amount of money he spends privately in order to support these programs. When the government enters the bond market to support these programs, there is a crowding out of investment in marginal industries, which are the ones most likely to hire young and unskilled workers. So the government employs one group of people through its action and makes another group of people unemployed.

I believe that the minimum wage law violates our constitutional right to make contracts. As a matter of fact, I have two proposed amendments to the Constitution that I would like to see Congressman Solarz take back with him. The first is "Everyone has the right to lower their price if they wish," and the second is "Everyone has the right to engage in voluntary exchanges without the sanction of a third party."

Much of the inflation and adjusting of the minimum wage is a direct result of government fostering inflation. In California, a man was arrested for selling milk at 15 cents lower than the approved price. Do you think it was an irate consumer who complained that the price was too low? Government activity forces up prices, then the government says, "Look at these poor people; let's raise the minimum wage so they can afford the price of things we forced up."

As to child labor legislation, there may have been some justification for a law that prohibited children from handling certain types of farm and factory machines back in the 1930s when such machines were in fact dangerous. But we have had technological advances, and certain types of machinery are much safer than they used to be. I think children have a constitutional right to work 40 hours per week if they want to. Now I would not like to see nine-year-olds working, and I would not like to see my nine-year-old daughter working, but if a parent decided that his nine-year-old should work, who am I to say that he should not be able to make that decision? Who am I to say what is good for you and your children? That is the person's responsibility, not the government's. I place a very high value on individual freedom.

The subminimum wage for youths will not produce the effect Congressman Solarz mentioned. In the Netherlands, France, Belgium, and Italy the youth differential is as much as 30 percent of the adult minimum wage, and a young person does not reach majority until he or she becomes twenty-two. In all those countries the unemployment rate for youths does not differ significantly from that of adults. For example, in Sweden from 1967 to 1968, the general rate of unemployment for the entire population was 2.6 percent, and the rate of youth unemployment was 3.9 percent. For Belgium in that period, the figures are similar, and in Italy, the unemployment rate for the general population was 3.5 percent, with the youth rate at 5.9 percent. These are all industrial countries, and we have not seen the cataclysmic effect of adults being unemployed as a result of the subminimum wage. I think that in these countries the people recognize that young workers are less skilled than older workers, and employers take that into consideration. With countries similar to our level of industrialization that do not have youth differentials in the minimum wage, unemployment among youths as compared with adults is similar to the ratio in the United States. So I would not necessarily accept the cataclysmic effects hypothesis of the youth differential.

Finally, Congressman Solarz mentioned the horrible sweatshop conditions of our earlier periods. All those early immigrants who came to our cities years ago and who went through those sweatshops are now our high- and middle-income people. They had a chance to get a foothold in the system. Those who were denied the sweatshop opportunity are now our low-income and hard-core unemployed people.

Stephen Solarz's Rebuttal

I think that the heart of Professor Williams's case is that whatever the other advantages of the minimum wage may be, it works to the disadvantage of young people, who are denied jobs because we have established a minimum wage that makes it uneconomical for employers to put them on the payroll. I want to deal directly with that contention in my rebuttal.

We in the Congress just completed a great debate on this issue. Many of my colleagues who argued as Professor Williams does contended that since the minimum wage hurts younger workers, it should be amended to establish a subminimum wage for youths, geared to 85 percent of the minimum wage for adults. This, it was proposed, was a way to make it economical to hire young people who would otherwise not be qualified for jobs. As far as I am aware, not a single member of Congress (let alone a single person of significance who testified before the committees that considered this legislation) argued that the way to deal with youth unemployment is to eliminate the minimum wage completely. The argument was to establish a subminimum wage (particularly for young people) in order to give the disadvantaged an advantage that they would not otherwise have.

I think that the subminimum wage is a bad idea for several reasons. First, had it been put into effect, the result would have been the substitution of young people for slightly older workers on the payrolls of the firms that hire them. While it would have undoubtedly reduced the number of young people who are unemployed, it would have increased the number of people who are receiving the minimum wage and would have added to the ranks of the unemployed people from those categories. And who are the people who are today earning the minimum wage? The greatest percentage is young people and minorities. So we would have had a situation in which young people who were laid off as a result of the minimum wage would have been hired at the expense of people who otherwise would have had jobs.

Second, in a slack economy such as ours, a subminimum wage would have resulted not in any net increase in employment, but rather in a reshuffling of those who were already employed. A few more young people would have gotten jobs, and a few more slightly older people would have lost jobs. Obviously, if an employer can hire someone to do a job at 20 cents an hour cheaper, he would do so.

Third, a subminimum wage fails to take into account that while a number of young people would have been given jobs that they otherwise could not have gotten, an increase in the minimum wage would increase the salaries of millions of young people who are in the minimum wage category. In other words, if there are several thousand who would lose their jobs because of the increased minimum wage, there are 4.5 million Americans, many of whom are young, whose wages would increase because of the increase in the minimum wage. In making those kinds of tradeoffs, we have to weigh one factor against another.

Fourth, an increased minimum wage generates more consumption, which in turn generates more jobs. This result benefits young people who otherwise would not get jobs. For every person who loses a job because of an increased minimum wage, other people get jobs because of the increased demand and employment.

Fifth, I suggest that the way to deal with this problem of youth unemployment is the way Congress attempted to deal with it during the last session—by passing legislation to establish job training and job creation programs for young people. We just appropriated $1 billion to generate 1.3 million jobs in the public and private sectors for young people who otherwise would be unemployed.

Who oppose this legislation? The very people who are against the minimum wage on the grounds that it hurts young people. If in fact the minimum wage works to the disadvantage of young people and minorities, why are the Urban League, the NAACP, and other civil rights organizations in favor of increasing the minimum wage? They recognize that, on balance, the people, constituencies, and interests they represent are better served by an increased minimum wage and a rejection of the subminimum wage. Although some people may suffer from an increased minimum wage, society as a whole, including young people and minorities, is better off by increasing rather than eliminating the minimum wage.

Let us assume that some teenagers are deprived of jobs because of the minimum wage and that these teenagers would have jobs if the minimum wage were eliminated. Would it be better for society if these teenagers replace people who have families to support? I am not prepared to argue that society profits when a teenager with no responsibilities is given a job preference over a breadwinner. However, I do not want the teenager to suffer either, so I think that the answer is government programs—the kind that were adopted during the last session of Congress. Paradoxically, these programs were opposed by the same people who were against the minimum wage on the ground that it harms young people.

I do not think that one can sustain the argument that an increased minimum wage has had an inflationary impact. In fact, it is just the opposite: increased inflation has resulted in an increased minimum wage to allow workers to catch up with inflation. (If we look at the historical statistics correlating increases in the minimum wage with increases in the cost of living during the year following the increased minimum wage, we find that the increases in the cost of living have been approximately 1 percent.)

My definition of labor value is based on common sense. In determining how much to pay people, the employer obviously must take into account many factors. However, I think that the most significant is the going wage for a comparable position, with the going wage being more or less established by the market in the surrounding community. If employers can hire someome for $3 an hour, that is one thing, but if someone comes along and says, "I'll do it for $2 because I need the work," the employer will obviously hire that person. Thus, rather than get hung up on how to define true value, which I think is a very technical economic question, I believe that we should look at the real consequences of eliminating the minimum wage.

Unemployment is a function of several factors, and even those who contend that the minimum wage contributes to unemployment would not argue that it is the sole cause. In attempting to analyze the impact of the minimum wage on unemployment, one has to untangle it conceptually from other contributing factors. And here I think that it is relevant to point out that the Fair Labor Standards Act requires the Secretary of Labor periodically to analyze the impact of the minimum wage on unemployment. All such reports have concluded that no evidence exists to attribute any increased unemployment to an increased minimum wage. Although increased unemployment may have occurred during the period when the minimum wage was increased, this pattern was not necessarily cause and effect. Remember that the minimum wage increase that recently became effective applied to 4.5 million workers out of a labor force of 94 million people—a relatively small percentage.

Of course I do not want to suggest that even at $2.65 an hour some people do not lose their jobs as a result of employers having to pay a wage that to them is no longer productive. I suspect, however, that as you go up the ladder from $2.65 to $5, the consequences do become catastrophic. At the present level, though, I think that the benefits far outweigh the disadvantages. If we eliminated the minimum wage completely, I have no doubt that there would be many more people working, but they would be working at wages that would not enable them to maintain a minimum decent standard of living. As it is, the minimum wage does not enable many people to reach the federally defined minimum poverty level. In an economy in which almost 7 million people are out of work, it is unreasonable to argue that a youth differential would result in a substantial increase in youth employment without resulting in increased unemployment among older workers.

One of the great tragedies of our country is that 7 million men and women want work but cannot find jobs. I think that everybody has a right to work, and I think that it is the responsibility of government to adopt programs that will put people to work productively if those jobs cannot be provided in the normal functioning of the private sector. In the part of the country that I am from, there is a lot of useful work that could be done by people who are presently unemployed, and I would much rather see people on payrolls than on welfare rolls. For every 1 percent of unemployment, we are losing $16 billion to $17 billion on such things as unemployment insurance and welfare payments. I would much rather use that money to put people to work doing things that are socially useful, and at a wage that would enable them to maintain a decent standard of living.

Professor Williams referred to a report by Secretary Marshall indicating that 90,000 jobs would be lost to young people if the minimum wage were increased. However, 4.5 million workers benefited directly from an increased minimum wage, and many of these workers are young and members of minority groups. As a matter of fact, while blacks constitute 11 percent of the work force as a whole, they constitute 17 percent of the work force earning the minimum wage. So here are people who directly benefit from an increase in the minimum wage. Moreover, an undefined number of people who were able to get jobs have an increase in purchasing power made possible by the increase in the minimum wage. I think that a raised standard of living for 4.5 million Americans and their families outweighs the loss of jobs for 90,000 people.

Professor William's position on child labor tends to discredit some of the other arguments he has been offering. I think that there is a clear consensus in our society that it is simply inappropriate for young children at the ages of eight or nine, who should be getting an education, to spend 40 hours a week in factories or sweatshops because they may be unfortunate enough to have parents who want to extract as much financial benefit as they can from their children. I think that as a society we have a responsibility to look out for our children's welfare, and if a consequence of Professor William's ideology is to create a situation in which children will waste their young lives away in order to earn a little extra money for their parents, his is a philosophy that most Americans would find difficult to accept.

If as a result of minimum wage legislation, people are paid more than they otherwise would receive, the incremental increase in their wages will generate a concomitant increase in their demand for goods. In order to satisfy that demand, production will have to increase, and in order to satisfy that increase, employment will have to increase as well. In fact, when legislated increases occur, millions of Americans benfit without losing their jobs. Somehow I think that there is a suggestion here that everytime you increase the minimum wage, everyone who has been getting the minimum wage is thrown out of work because his or her employer cannot afford to pay the increase. Actually, the opposite is true: the overwhelming majority of people who receive the minimum wage when there is a legislated increase get the benefit of that increase and also keep their jobs. Given the fact that the minimum wage accords people annual incomes below the poverty level, we are talking about millions of Americans whose lives are significantly benefited by the increased minimum wage and who live a little better as the result of it.

In many states, people remain significantly better off working at the minimum wage than being on welfare. Thus, if we eliminate the minimum wage, millions of working people in this country who are unorganized and without the benefits of collective bargaining would witness a significant decline in earnings. This decline would be catastrophic for those living at the margin of existence.

3

Should the Right of Collective Bargaining and Strike Be Extended to Public Employees?

Donald T. Weckstein and
Jake Garn

Donald T. Weckstein's Presentation

It is my position that the right of public employees to engage in collective bargaining, including a limited right to strike, is theoretically justified, consistent with free-market principles, and feasible (but not inevitable) and desirable for society. I begin by setting forth reasons for allowing collective bargaining in the public sector. At least since 1935, private-sector employees have enjoyed a right to organize, engage in concerted activities (including the right to strike), and participate in collective bargaining through representatives of their choosing. While this system is not perfect and has been subject to some criticism, it generally has worked well and has been accepted as an institution that is preferable to other probable alternatives. For example, collective bargaining is judged superior to unilateral decision making by employers, government control, or some form of socialism. Collective bargaining has the desirable quality of involving those to be affected by a decision in the decision-making process.

Why, therefore, should collective bargaining not apply to public-sector employees? Is there something unique about those who have their paychecks signed by a government rather than by a private employer? Obviously, there are differences, but there are also differences between men and women; yet we now recognize that each is entitled to be treated equally under the law unless their biological differences merit some unique treatment. So it should be with public employees. To the extent that there are differences, the law ought to take them into account; to the extent that there are no differences, there is no reason why we should not have the same type of laws that apply to the private sector.

Let us briefly examine some of the alleged differences that are suggested in political speeches, scholarly writings, and the like. We start off with the concept that the public employer is different because it is "the sovereign." To me, this is just a bootstrap argument that merely restates the question. The question being Should the fact that the employer is the sovereign make a difference? Thus the argument is not meaningful unless we go a step further and say that because the public employer is the sovereign, it should be immune from ordinary labor laws on the theory that "the king can do no wrong.'' However, this common-law doctrine has been discredited because of the inappropriateness of this royal notion to modern society and because equity and fairness require that even governments be held accountable. The federal government and the courts and legislators of most states have drastically curtailed sovereign immunity and recognized governmental liability for its torts and contracts. A collective bargaining agreement is a contract that can bind a government just as it is bound by the obligation of its other contracts. Furthermore, modern governments have gone far beyond the restrictive functions that were performed by governments at the time of the adoption of sovereign immunity. When governments undertake proprietary and commercial type activities, the courts recognize that they must be held accountable to the same extent as would private citizens or entities performing similar functions.

It is sometimes suggested that public employees must remain loyal to their government and accept unilateral determination of wages and working conditions because they are employees of a sovereign. In light of the experiences we have had recently with Watergate, the Imperial Presidency, and the Vietnam war, it does not seem tenable to assert that a public employee is being disloyal simply because he or she questions the actions or seeks input into the decisions of government.

A more formidable reason for distinguishing between public- and private-sector employees is that government services may be essential and that we cannot allow an interruption (particularly by way of a strike) in the flow of those services to the public who demands them. However, the fact that the employee is on the government payroll hardly makes that person's service essential. We must look at the particular function being exercised. Certain police, fire, and health services performed by governmental employees may be considered essential, but the modern state has gone far beyond these traditional safety and health functions to perform many other services for ''the general welfare'' that had been previously, and often still are, performed by private-sector enterprises. It would be ludicrous to maintain that mowing the grass at municipal golf courses, or maintaining the town swimming pool, or providing assistance at public libraries is more essential because performed by public employees than the services of privately owned electric utilities, transit corporations, or telephone companies. The question of whether we can tolerate an interruption in a service should depend not on whether it is performed by a public or private employee, but on whether its curtailment would substantially harm public health and safety. Even if a ban on strikes by public employees performing essential services can be justified, it does not necessarily follow that these employees must be denied the right to engage in other aspects of collective bargaining. Moreover, even some essential or important governmental functions could be cut off, curtailed, or delayed from time to time without serious harm to the public.

Society probably could survive very well at least a short-run interruption in public legal education or the distribution of parking tickets.

Present-day federal, state, and local governments, under whatever political party, no longer limit themselves to the performance of those functions which cannot be performed at all or as well by private enterprise, rather they engage in many activities the public could survive without, or at least without having the government perform them.

More significantly, some distinguished scholars have contended that while economic market constraints may effectively limit runaway collective bargaining in the private sector, they have no similar application to the public sector. Economic theory and recent political history do not support this proposition. The theory of "derived demand" suggests that the power of a union to force a favorable settlement is derived from the demand for the product that is being produced and marketed.[1] As interpreted by Albert Rees, the theory says that a union's power increases with (1) the presence of an inelastic demand for the ultimate product (in the public sector, that would be the services performed by government), (2) the strategic importance of labor in the production of that product, (3) the relative smallness of the percentage of the cost that labor constitutes of the total cost of the product, and (4) the nonavailability of alternatives for that product or the labor producing that product.[2] If we look at some of these factors as applied to public employment, we do find that some of the constraints that would be available in the private sector would be less available in the public sector. In the private sector, if you have an elastic demand and higher wages are sought, which increase the total cost of the product to the consumer, the consumer will switch to other products or manufacturers. This reduces the sales of the original products, which causes the employer to curtail his labor force (so that higher wages constitute a tradeoff for fuller employment) or improve technology or economize in some other manner so that he can continue to stay in business. This scenario thus constitutes a strong economic basis for resisting unreasonable wage demands. How much of this applies in the public sector?

Inelasticity of demand for government services is generally assumed. After all, government has no competitors in performing its services, or does it? More and more, we are recognizing that there are limits to which the price of government services can be carried, and with government expansion into nonessential areas, there are many governmental services that can be successfully performed by private enterprise. Indeed, but for the fact that rival postal services are prohibited by law, it has been demonstrated that private enterprise can more efficiently operate a postal service than can the government. Currently, there are businesses that deliver parcels more quickly than does the federal mail service. There is also private competition with government in education (especially postsecondary), recreation, sanitation, and garbage collection. There are even private fire departments in some cities, supported by subscription rather than tax collection. So it is possible that if the price of even traditional government services becomes too high, private enterprise will move in and successfully compete. A government also can contract out many of its services. This is done commonly, for example, with highway construction. Most of the workers building highways are not employees of government, but of private independent contractors. Thus, when wage costs accelerate, the government may have to abandon some peripheral service, contract out certain functions, or curtail basic services, as has been the case, for example, in mail deliveries. New York City eliminated 38,000 employees, or 13 percent of its work force, in the midst of its fiscal crisis in 1975.

The second factor determining derived demand is the importance of labor to the ultimate product. Labor is very important to governmental functions. Labor costs generally constitute 62 percent of local government budgets and 40 percent of the cost of state governments. This means that labor is of strategic importance to the performance of government services, but it also means that labor costs cannot be hidden easily in the total product. Thus the third factor, the relative percentage of labor costs of total costs, suggests a decreased power for organized labor in the public sector. Since labor costs do constitute an extremely high percentage of the cost of the total government services, a governmental employer is unlikely to readily give in to demands for higher wages because it is more clearly accountable for paying additional wages or other economic benefits. A likely, and unpopular, result will be higher taxes and a lower political life expectancy for the responsible public officeholders.

In a provocative book, Harry Wellington and Ralph Winters take issue with the fact that taxation is an effective method of curtailing wages in the public sector, at least not as effective as would be consumer options in the private sector.[3] Their argument is basically that taxation is too remote from the time in which wage increases are given and that its impact is too diffuse to be recognized by the taxpayer as the reason for having to pay higher taxes when wages or other economic benefits of public employees are raised. Wellington also argues that the public official, instead of being concerned with economic constraints, is more concerned with political constraints, and that it is good politics to give in to union demands. He claims that if the official hopes to be reelected, or aspires to higher office, he is more likely to be successful by giving in to the union than by fighting it. This may have been the lessons of the 1960s, but it clearly is not the lesson of the 1970s. Indeed, witness San Diego Mayor Pete Wilson and those politicians who have opposed strong union demands and have made great political capital. California's Proposition 13 epitomizes the taxpayer revolt, while in referenda in San Francisco, San Diego, Santa Barbara, Oakland, and other cities around the country, people strongly voted against organized labor's positions in the public sector. So it seems to me that the opposite is true today, that it is not good politics to give in to higher wage demands (at least those which can be considered beyond productivity increases). The political leaders now have a victim, the labor unions, to blame for the financial conditions of cities and the increases in taxes. It may be politically more desirable for a public official to allow the public-service employees to strike than to give in to demands that appear excessive. While there may not be competative governments serving the same area, disgruntled taxpayers can vote out those government leaders who raise taxes or the taxpayers can move to communities with a lower tax burden.

Some may point to New York City, where increased labor costs (particularly in pension funds) was one of the reasons for the virtual bankruptcy of the city. This may have been true, but nevertheless, New York City need not be the vision of the future for San Diego or other communities. On the contrary, the example of urban sprawl in Los Angeles has been used to gain support for contained-growth policies in San Diego. Likewise, city officials throughout the country are using the example of New York (and other cities that are either in bankruptcy or on the verge of it) for refusing to give in to what they consider to be exorbitant demands by public-employee unions. Thus there is little fear that our politicians will capitulate to unions because of possible reprisals at the polls. Moreover, in many states there are legal as well as political restrictions on deficit financing and the power to tax and borrow.

Another argument, on which Wellington and Winters put much weight is the fear that allowing public employees to engage in collective bargaining will distort the political process because it will give them two bites at the apple (or if you would prefer a sports analogy, it allows them to perform an end run around the bargaining team to whomever holds the political power in a community). In other words, public employees get to bargain with a representative of the executive at the local, state, or federal level, and if they do not get what they want, they go to the legislature and seek to get it there. Because of this additional opportunity, it is said that public employees have more political power than do other interest groups who may have equally meritorious claims to make on government funds. Some would argue that this is undesirable; others would argue that it is merited. For example, Clyde Summers has said that the additional power is needed by public employees because every interest group is aligned against public employees when it comes to increasing their economic benefits.[4] The taxpayers are certainly against it, and all the other interest groups that are looking for money from the government are against it because of the fear that what goes to the public employees will not go to them. Since the public employees clearly have a larger stake in their own salary than any other interest group,

Summers suggests that it is only fair that they be given this additional political leverage.

In noneconomic areas, however, both Wellington and Summers seem to agree that public-employee bargaining may well distort policy making. For example, an issue of educational policy such as should the public schools be decentralized is of interest both to employees and to other interest groups. But if those other interest groups are not represented at the bargaining table, any decision affecting them may be unfair. This situation can be controlled in one of several ways. One way is to simply limit the scope of bargaining so as to exclude those items from collective bargaining. Another is to have multilateral bargaining, whereby representatives of these other groups are present and engage in the bargaining when issues of interest to them come up.

Another argument against allowing public employees to collective bargain derives from the problem of trying to identify with whom they should bargain. Who is the employer? Is it the executive who supervises the employees or the legislature which pays the bill? Or on the city level, is it the mayor, the city manager, or the city council that votes to adopt the budget and appropriate the funds? This is a very difficult question with which to deal. However, it does not mean that we should not bargain at all. We could create an arrangement in which the legislative authority is represented at the bargaining table (such as exists in Wisconsin, where they have formed the Joint Committee on Employment Relations (identified by its acronym, JOKER). Or we could allow the ultimate authority to be exercised by the legislative body, which could reject the results of a bargained contract and send everybody back to the bargaining table. This is not the best system, but neither is it a reason for denying collective bargaining by public employees.

Another argument against public sector bargaining is that government is engaged in a nonprofit enterprise. Well, so is much of the private sector (some of which was unintended). Hospitals and education are examples of nonprofit industries that have recently come under the jurisdiction of the National Labor Relations Act, and they do not seem to be suffering unduly because of it. The fact that one is engaged in nonprofit employment is not a reason by itself for saying that one should not be subject to collective bargaining.

Finally, there is the argument that we need to safeguard the rights of public employees through Civil Service on the merit principle or some other form of paternalism. I would suggest to you, as President Carter and the Congress have recognized, that Civil Service (at least on the federal level) is not working that well, and it could probably be said that on the state and municipal level the merit principle is not followed in many cases. Under Civil Service, it is extremely difficult to promote people solely on the basis of merit as opposed to seniority, or hire competent people from the outside rather than relying on promotions from within, or to get rid of incompetent people. I would suggest that collective bargaining, whereby just cause is required for discharge (which ultimately can be adjudicated before an impartial arbitrator) and promotions are typically made on the basis of seniority only where ability is equal, would be a better system than we have under Civil Service. But the existence of collective bargaining does not necessarily mean the end of Civil Service. They can exist together, both at the federal level and in states and cities. Despite all the inroads made on the authority of Civil Service Commissions, they still retain much of their original purpose of insulating public employees from politics in terms of employment, promotion, and discharge.

Collective bargaining in the public sector is consistent with free enterprise. Justice Oliver Wendell Holmes, Jr., while sitting on the Massachusetts Supreme Judicial Court, wrote in a minority opinion that even if free competition injures some, it benefits the overall good and is worth more to society than it costs. The policy of allowing free competition, he stated, "justifies the intentional infliction of temporal damage, including the damage of interference with a man's business, . . . when the damage is done not for its own sake, but as an instrumentality in reaching the end of victory in the battle of trade." Holmes noted that the competitive system justifies the self-interested actions of labor as well as capital, and that the free enterprise system is not limited to struggles of members in the same class. "One of the eternal conflicts out of which life is made up," he stated, "is that between the effort of every man to get the most he can for his services, and that of society, disguised under the name of capital, to get his services for the least possible return. Combination on the one side is patent and powerful. Combination on the other hand is the necessary and desirable counterpart, if the battle is to be carried on in a fair and equal way."[5] While Holmes was addressing himself to the private sector (and while there are other opinions of his that indicate some hostility to organized labor activities in the public sector, I think they have since become dated by subsequent developments), there is no more reason to trust government paternalism in the public sector than that of nongovernmental employees in the private sector. If we believe in self-interest as an effective method for the regulation of business, why should we not have confidence in the desirability of self-interest in the area of labor relations? As noted, government has infringed on more areas that compete with private business, and if public employee unions are too successful in their efforts to raise pay and economic benefits, they may force government to relinquish some of these areas back to private enterprise, which, I assume, would not disturb anyone believing in the free enterprise system.

Not only is public-employee collective bargaining theoretically justified, but it exists and it works. There are over thirty states that have legislation allowing collective bargaining in one form or another, and there are about sixty local ordinances that authorize it. In virtually all states, with or without legislation, public-employee collective bargaining is going on without serious interruptions in public services or the bankruptcy of governmental units.

Twenty percent of the work force is employed by one level or another of government. To tell these 15 million employees that they are not entitled to the organizational and bargaining rights of their counterparts employed by private enterprise seems to violate concepts of fairness and equality. The ABA Labor Law Section Committee on Labor Relations of Government Employees stated back in 1955 that: "A government which imposes upon other employers certain obligations in dealing with their employees may not in good faith refuse to deal with its own public servants on a reasonably similar favorable basis, modified, of course, to meet the exigencies of the public service. It should set the example for industry by being perhaps more considerate than the law requires of private enterprise."[6] Mayor David Vann of Birmingham, Alabama (coming from a part of the country not known for its liberalism) said in 1976 with respect to the question of whether public employees should have the right to engage in collective bargaining, "The right of a man to have an input on the conditions of his employment as represented through the traditional development of the labor system in our country, is a vital thing not only to human dignity but also to good employee morale."[7] Good decision making is sensitive to the interests of those affected by the decisions. The best assurance of such sensitivity is to let those affected by the decision become a part of the decision-making process. This is what collective bargaining does with respect to wages and conditions of employment, and it is as desirable and feasible for public employees as for those employed in the private sector.

Let us consider now the right to strike in the public sector. While there may still be a few recalcitrants who reject the entire concept of collective bargaining in the public sector, the reservations of most well-meaning people concern the fear of strikes by public employees. In my opinion, this fear is unnecessarily exaggerated and largely misplaced. Moreover, the outlawing of public-employee strikes seems to have little or no impact on their occurrence and serves mainly to make settlements more difficult to achieve and bring the law into disrepute.

Despite the fact that most state or local governments prohibit public employees from striking—even where collective bargaining is otherwise authorized—the incidence of strikes in jurisdictions is no less than in the few places where governmental employees enjoy a limited right to strike. Included in this latter category are the states of Alaska, Hawaii, Minnesota, Montana, Oregon, Pennsylvania, Rhode Island, and Vermont. It is true that one of these states, Pennsylvania, has had more strikes in recent years than any other state. But the next highest honors (or horrors) for most strikes go to Michigan, Ohio, California, Illinois, New York, Washington, and New Jersey, all of which prohibit public-employee strikes (with varying levels of enforcement). By contrast, Hawaii, one of the first jurisdictions to provide by statute for a limited right to strike, has had only one public employee strike.[8] One suspects that the incidence of strikes by public employees has more to do with population density, union militancy, labor relations history, and economic conditions than with the existence or prohibition of a right to strike. Indeed, there is some evidence of a positive correlation between the harshness of penalties for striking and the number of strikes occurring. For example, there have been more public-employee strikes in New York since the penalties were increased (to perhaps unrealistic levels including discharge and no raises for 3 years if rehired) by the Condon-Wadlin Act than occurred under the old Taylor law, which more realistically provided for fines and double-docking for illegal strikes. As a practical matter, courts are reluctant to enforce overly harsh penalties, which tarnishes the image of the law and its administration, and workers and their representatives more strongly resist settlement of the underlying labor dispute unless it also includes amnesty from penalties for illegal striking. Thus the outlawing of the strike just adds an unwelcome and divisive issue to public-employee collective bargaining, and more important, it does not prevent strikes.

The extreme position of outlawing all public-employee strikes, therefore, should—like the unrealistic and unworkable liquor prohibition—be discarded in favor of more feasible and effective regulation. The touchstone for such regulation should be whether a particular strike constitutes a danger to the health, safety, or essential welfare of the public. Thus distinctions will be made between strikes by police and firefighters, which may be preemptorily prohibited except as regards nonessential duties (for example, issuing bicycle licenses and giving parking tickets), and work stoppages by municipal golf course or state liquor store employees. In some cases, a strike, for example, by teachers or garbage collectors (although they are not the same for all purposes), may not initially threaten the public health, safety, or essential welfare, but it may do so if it becomes prolonged. A court or appropriate public-employee relations board could make the judgment as to when the line has been crossed.

In any event, as is the case with the legislation in those states which have expressly recognized a limited right to strike for public employees, no strike should be permitted until other dispute settlement procedures such as mediation, factfinding, and advisory arbitration have been exhausted. While time does not permit an analysis of the problems thought to be involved in allowing public officials to delegate decisions affecting employee relations to arbitrators, it is safe to conclude that this non-delegation doctrine finds little support in modern jurisprudence. Serious consideration should be given to allowing a governmental unit and representatives of its employees to voluntarily refer interest disputes over the terms of a new contract to arbitration and to requiring arbitration of disputes with those employees who are prohibited from striking. As of 1977, seventeen states have provided for compulsory arbitration in such cases. Although there is no evidence that arbitrators have acted irresponsibly or ignored economic realities in deciding interest disputes (with one or two notable exceptions), the discretion of the arbitrators could be limited by legislative promulgating of specific standards for decision, or by requiring the arbitrator to select one or the other party's final offer, or perhaps rejecting both if neither is in the public interest and remanding the dispute to the parties, or adopting the recommendations of a factfinder. This "last offer" arbitration procedure minimizes the intrusion of third-party policy choices into collective bargaining and tends to encourage realistic negotiations.

Should strikes still occur when only those which actually threaten the public health and safety are prohibited, the sanctions for the offending unions and workers should be reasonable and realistic, so that courts will not be reluctant to enforce them. Examples might include daily fines for the union and loss of some seniority for the employees, with a possibility of permanent replacement after due notice.

The great concern by both unions and the public with the right of public employees to strike may well be overblown. While many unions regard the opportunity to strike as essential to free collective bargaining, the fact is that it is not as effective a weapon in the public sector as in the private one. Whereas a strike against a private employer shuts off production or sales and therefore income, a public-employee strike does not interfere with the collection of taxes. Thus the employees suffer loss of their wages, while the public employer reaps a revenue windfall without having to make budgeted expenditures for salaries of striking employees. Recent public-employee strikes have not resulted in wholesale capitulations by elected officials, and most state and local governments have survived the 300 or so public-employee strikes that occur annually with little more inconvenience than that caused by legal strikes of private employees. In some cases, a private-sector strike, such as in the coal or railroad industry, may present a more serious threat to the public than most public-sector strikes. Thus the issue in each case should be whether the strike endangers public health, safety, or essential welfare and not whether it involves public or private employees.

In conclusion, I hope that I have illustrated the wisdom of UCLA Professor Benjamin Aaron's observation that "The plain fact is that collective bargaining in the public sector is a reality; it is here to stay; it is, I believe, an irreversible process. Our job is not to prevent it, abolish it, or contain it. Rather, our job is to try to make it work better."[9]

Jake Garn's Presentation

The problem we are discussing is one that I long lived with. For 7 years as mayor of Salt Lake City I dealt with city employees, policemen, firemen, and their daily experiences. They are the infantry of government. My knowledge did not come from the Brookings Institute or Wellington and Winters and their theoretical conceptions but from the real world. What we did for our public employees in Salt Lake City concerning the necessity of collective bargaining and binding arbitration was to allow all employees the opportunity to speak to their elected officials. Any employee, not just selected union representatives, could come in and talk to us about wage packages or fringe benefits.

My answer to the question that was posed earlier is "Absolutely not." At the outset, let me say that I certainly do not quarrel with the constitutional right of public employees to organize and join unions if they so desire. I want to emphasize the phrase "If they so desire," because I believe very strongly that free people should have the right to decide whether or not they want to join a union. I believe that in the public sector, the matter of collective bargaining (a natural outgrowth of unionism) should be carefully considered. Every collective bargaining relationship depends on establishing an adversary relationship between employer and employee. This has happened in Salt Lake City. Since I stepped down as mayor, collective bargaining agreements have been instituted, and it is interesting how the good feeling that existed is now gone. There is now an adversary relationship, and many of the liberal things we did for our employees are a matter of contract. They gained a lot in that contract, but they lost a lot too. There is nothing but complaints anymore. When I go home, I always hear, "Mayor, you were right. Collective bargaining has not worked out. You just cannot walk into an administrator's office any more. Now it's, 'Go back to the terms of the contract and the letter of the law; boom! boom! boom! No flexibility! Let's argue about it next year!'"

Unions, in order to win and hold the loyalty of their members, must demand more than the employer is willing to offer. If the union were willing to accept only what the employer would be willing to offer, it would serve no useful purpose for its members and would have no support. A union, by its very nature, must make demands. The only instrument that the unions have at their disposal (particularly in the public sector) to gain support for their demands is the withdrawal of the services of their members. This simply means strike. Striking is the use of a coercive force and cannot be defined or construed in any other way.

This brings me to my central argument about collective bargaining and strikes in the public sector. They destroy the basic notions of sovereignty and accountability in our governmental institutions. Before I tell you why I believe this, let me make a point about the reasons we are here. What has led us to the point where we can actually discuss seriously the transfer of any of the functions and powers of the sovereign to a private and independent organization not subject to public control and rarely subject to public scrutiny? The answer can be found in the enormous growth of federal, state, and local governments. The Bureau of Labor Statistics estimates that public employment has grown faster than any other sector of the economy. There are now some 15 million government workers and 2½ million federal employees—and their numbers have grown by leaps and bounds.

Public-employee unions have discovered that unionism holds the most lucrative potential of all, and they are the fastest growing, best organized, and most militant unions in the country. Between 1951 and 1972, the government work force grew by 151 percent, payrolls grew by 596 percent, union membership by 130 percent, and strikes by public employees by 1,000 percent. Therefore, it is hardly surprising that Americans are taking a closer look at the national interest in labor relations in state, local, and federal government. As a result, several state legislatures have passed laws governing labor relations of public employees. What have we reaped? Legislators have usually been persuaded to adopt the orderly process of collective bargaining from the private sector.

Do you imagine that such laws are justified in the name of peace and tranquility? That is what they told me for 7 years. They kept saying, "We would not have these troubles every year, Mayor, if you would just agree to a written contract." I wish I could show you some Salt Lake City newspapers covering events of the last 3 years. You should read about all the peace and tranquility that has existed since they have had collective bargaining. There is a considerable difference. Union supporters had assured the public employer conjugal bliss and reduced industrial strife. Yet the facts overwhelmingly support the contrary. Virtually every solution has created more unionization problems than have been solved. Union unrest and illegal strikes continue to mount. Moreover, if the unions are not able to get concessions at the bargaining table, they frequently go to the state legislature or Congress. These solutions generally do nothing more than add to the power and privileges of the union organizers and do not benefit the rank and file members.

Prohibition of public employees from striking is sound in that it recognizes the unique position and potential ability of striking public servants to paralyze the community. However, the record shows that officials of the public-employee unions openly flout laws that stand as obstacles to their quest to take over control of services and then brag about their illegal actions. Seldom has this resulted in any significant legal penalties, mainly because of the fear of public officials that strong punishment will be met by even more retaliation. The attitudes of public union advocates justify concern about the impact of collective bargaining and strikes in the public sector.

In early November 1974, George Meany addressed a group of public employees and, among other things, said that although it is unlawful to strike in the Civil Service, an AFL-CIO tactic is to ignore such laws. Meany advised over 15 million civil servants to "quit working for the guy who's kicking you around. You stop the job, you shut it down, and you take the consequences. If the guy happens to be the mayor of the city or governor of the state, it doesn't make a damn bit of difference."[10]

What kind of leadership is that? What kind of service is that to the taxpayers of this country? What implications does this suggest for stable government and responsible civil servants who should be accountable to the voters and taxpayers who pay their wages?

I do not happen to be the only one shocked by these statements. *The New York Times*, subsequent to Meany's speech, said in an editorial: "The accent Mr. Meany chose to put on militant action to bring governors and mayors to heel—with or without a law—raises new doubts that the general welfare would benefit from a federal mandate to strengthen civil service unions."[11] And *The New York Times* is hardly known as a conservative newspaper.

On November 11, 1974, the *New York Daily News* editorialized as follows: "The 94th Congress must screw up its courage and make a firm stand against such reckless labor adventuring. Government workers are entitled to representation and bargaining. But strikes against the public good should be taboo—period. And that also goes for compulsory union representation."[12] We simply cannot afford these callous, indefensible threats to the health, safety, and economy of the nation, nor should civil service workers be compelled to pay tribute to unions to hold jobs that are won on merit.

These expressions of opposition to strikes in the public sector are not new. They have long been a matter of concern to those who understand that unionization leads to collective bargaining and collective bargaining must carry the expressed or implied threat of a strike. I am not one who quotes Franklin Delano Roosevelt very often, but in this case I'm going to. In a letter in 1937 to Luther Steward, President of the National Federation of Federal Employees, he said that "militant tactics have no place in the functions of any organization of Government employees. . . . [A] strike of public employees manifests nothing less than an intent on their part to prevent or obstruct the operation of Government until their demands are satisfied. Such action, looking toward the paralysis of Government by those who have sworn to support it, is unthinkable and intolerable.''[13] President Roosevelt also said in the same letter: ''[C]ollective bargaining, as usually understood, cannot be transplanted into the public service.'' Again, in my view, he was correct.

There are definite differences between the public sector and the private sector that make it impossible to have a system of collective bargaining that is developed in the private sector and functions in the public sector without doing great harm. First of all, the government is a monopoly. There is not, and there cannot be, competition with government in most of its activities. There are those who argue that government is engaged in many activities in direct competition with the private sector. However, rather than being an argument against these activities in government (and I agree completely with Dean Weckstein), there are a lot of activities at every level of government.

One thing I want to stand up and applaud is his statement that there are a lot of government services we ought to turn back to the private sector. (Look how beautifully we have run the post office.) Now, we (the federal government) propose to get involved in offshore drilling, since we are so expert at that. We will do a magnificent job there too. So there we completely agree that there are a lot of public services we ought to get rid of at the government level.

I do not think, however, that anyone would question the necessity of a government monopoly on national defense, law enforcement, judicial proceedings, taxation, and a long list of functions that belong entirely to the people through the aegis of their elected representatives. Second, in government as opposed to the private sector, there is no profit motive. The economic theorists may theorize on the profit motive situation, but look at their results. Across this country, government continually raises taxes to cover its mistakes, inefficiency, and mismanagement.

We have planned a half-trillion dollar budget with a $62 million deficit this year. Businesses do not have this luxury; they reach a point of diminishing return, where prices go up to a point and people stop buying. Yes there are taxpayer protests, and we defeat tax increases in bond elections. But the majority of taxes are not subject to our will, except through our elected representatives. The government simply covers its mistakes and inefficiencies by increasing your taxes and cutting services. Businesses cannot do that; they will go bankrupt. New York City is still in existence despite its actual bankruptcy.

I regard the profit motive as one of the single most important forces giving America its tremendous productive capacity. Dean Weckstein mentioned that this is the very heart of our competitive free enterprise system. The profit motive is absent from considerations in government-employee relations. If it were not absent, I would guarantee you that there would be thousands and thousands fewer employees in government. I can think of 10,000 government employees in Washington who you would never miss. You would probably get more work done if they were gone, because they would not be stumbling all over each other. But if we pay our public officials less money, not one cent of that money goes into our pockets. Our position is that of every other public body: to provide the necessary services to the people in the best and most efficient manner possible. To provide this service, we must employ people, and the better people we hire, the better service we can provide.

Thus it is in the public interest to hire only the very best public employees. In order to do this, we must be ever mindful that total compensation and working conditions for public employees must be comparable with the conditions in the private sector, or we are not going to have capable, competent employees in government. Now we come to the most crucial difference between public and private employment, and this is the nature of government itself. The ruling principle in the private sector is free contract; that is, every action that takes place between free individuals and free society is done by mutual agreement. This is true in employment, in purchasing, and in all our obligations. However, the ruling principle of government is authority, and it alone has the power to make decisions providing a sensible ordered society. Government has the authority to provide police, fire, garbage, water, and sewer services. It can be demonstrated that the intrusion of collective bargaining and the right to strike in the public sector are serious challenges to the orderly process of government.

Consider some of the following facts: the first compulsory public-sector collective bargaining law in the United States was enacted in Wisconsin in 1959. At the end of 1958, membership in the public-sector unions throughout the United States was over 1 million. There were only fifteen strikes against the government in 1958. By the end of 1974, thirty-eight states had enacted one form or another of compulsory bargaining legislation. The membership in public-sector unions had increased to over 5½ million, and there were 382 strikes against government. Pennsylvania is a good example of the cause-and-effect relationship between public- and private-sector bargaining laws and increasing strike activity. In the 12-year period prior to the state's passage of the public-sector compulsory collective bargaining law, there were seventy-two strikes, or an average of six per year. In the 4 years after the passage of the law, there were 292 strikes, or 73 per year. Every state except one that passed a compulsory collective bargaining law in the public sector has seen increased strike activity. Taking all states into account, it is clear that the average number of public-employee strikes increased fourfold after legislation was passed to provide for public-sector collective bargaining. All but seven of those states had statutes prohibiting strikes. This is exactly what George Meany said, law does not mean very much to a striker.

An example or two will give you a better idea than these statistics that collective bargaining in the public sector leads inevitably to strikes. In July 1974, Baltimore had an illegal garbage strike, and stinking refuse filled the streets. Rioters took over and looted and burned stores in actions similar to the racial riots of 1968. Unions harassed private collectors and volunteers trying to remove the stench from the cities. Picket lines were placed around the city landfills, and car windows were smashed when private citizens tried to remove their own trash and deliver it to the garbage dumps themselves. The private sector was trying to take over the situation, but the unions were not allowing it. Jerry Wurf, International President of the American Federation of State, County, and Municipal Employees, whose local called the strike, warned Governor Mandel that Baltimore would burn to the ground unless the city gave in to his demands. As an aftermath of the strike, and because of apparent political reprisals by labor, Governor Mandel said, "I am amazed that an irresponsible outside union leader like Mr. Wurf could come into the state of Maryland and threaten me with political reprisal for a problem that was of his own doing."[14] The illegal strike, violence, and intimidation tied the city into knots for 16 days.

Kansas City firefighters illegally struck in the fall of 1975, attempting to receive what that they asserted was a parity in salary with policemen. The strike ended after 4 days of bitterness and an accusation by the mayor and other city officials that members of the firefighters' union had set some of the 200 blazes that had erupted during the strike. The number of fires reported was high, above average; volunteers and national guard and city employees struggled to keep the city from going out of control. Some of the volunteers who answered calls came with fire extinguishers loaded with diesel fuel.

In 1975, a state of emergency was delared in San Francisco after a night of robberies and scattered violence when a bomb exploded outside the residence of Mayor Alioto. Policemen had defied a court order to return to work. The city fire fighters then joined the striking policemen and withdrew protection from the city's international airport. Transit workers also threatened to join the strike. This is in a city where the starting wage for a police cadet or firefighter was $16,440 per year (when I made only $19,000 as full-time mayor of Salt Lake City). Firefighters were striking, causing all these problems in San Francisco, and I had the responsibility of running a city with a $50 million budget for $3,000 more per year? Mayor Alioto invoked his emergency powers to override San Francisco's Board of Supervisors decision to raise starting salaries to $18,860. The settlement also provided administrative amnesty for any law violations that the strikers committed, including violating a court order enjoining the police to go back to work. It is estimated that under the new contract the average city expenditure per officer including fringe benefits is $29,450.

It is not difficult to see from these examples what happens when public employees defy citizens, taxpayers, and elected officials. Some identifiable results are loss of control of the political processes to union officials, disrupted services, and loss of necessary services, such as police and fire protection. It is not a matter of being without electrical power or a car, it is your life and your health. When I speak of essential services, which involve your life and your health, public employees should not have the right to deny them to you.

I wonder why the government employment is so bad in this country when over 5 million people applied to the federal government last year for only a few thousand jobs. In Salt Lake City, I never had trouble finding employees; the police and fire departments had waiting lists at all levels. If government employment is so terrible, why do they line up and wait to get into it in the first place?

Withholding fire protection results in increased fire and fire hazards, increased insurance rates (which taxpayers pay), and the loss of many less important services. Some say that these results are due to a lack of response by city or state officials to meet the demands of the unions. Well I am sure that there are cases in this country where mayors and governors are not as fair as they should be, but the people have the right and opportunity to determine through the elective process who their leaders will be. If public employees are being abused, they can take their case to the people, without having to resort to the threat and intimidation of strike and disruption of essential services.

This is a pretty old-fashioned idea—getting rid of the mayor and the senator at the ballot box if you do not like the job being done. Tell me, how do you get rid of the international vice president of the public-employee union?

New York City is a classic example of a city that has totally surrendered to unions. I am forced to conclude that the reason for New York's fiscal problem is its total sellout to the public-service unions. Most of the union members earn more for menial jobs than I earned being mayor of Salt Lake City. If I, as mayor of Salt Lake City, wanted to provide the same number of public employees in proportion to the population as New York has (adjusting education from the hypothetical; Salt Lake City has a separate educational system), I would have had to increase the budget by 900 percent, from $30 million a year to $270 million. How long can this sort of thing go on? The abuses in wage rates and pension funds are an unbelievable assortment of horror stories. Do you know, by the way, that New York City has a budget higher than the next twenty-three cities combined? That list includes Chicago, Philadelphia, Los Angeles, San Francisco, and Houston. The garbage collectors in New York make more than the mayor of Salt Lake City.

As Rees and Wellington say, the power of municipal unions could elect the mayor of any city, because of their organizational capabilities coupled with the generally low voter turnout. Municipal unions constitute a minority that can become a majority. The final report of the temporary Commission on City Finance appointed by Mayor Beame in 1975 pointed out that the specific labor regulations structure mandated by collective bargaining laws substantially lessens the city's degree of control over labor costs and personnel management. This has fragmented the mayoral managerial authority and weakened the cities influence because mutual arbitrators can settle disputes in a binding manner. A series of Republican and Democratic mayors just sold out.

Third-party arbitrators have the power to make decisions that affect the cost of government, taxes, and the quality and quantity of public service. But they do not have the accountability that accompanies elective office. When I was mayor of Salt Lake City, I was required by the Utah constitution to balance the budget every year or go to jail. I had the responsibility to do that every year, and I was accountable to the voters if I did not. But if you have binding arbitration with a third party dictating wages and fringe benefits that go beyond the revenues provided, who raises the taxes? Not the elected officials, but some out-of-state person the people never hear of and cannot put out of power. The accountability is not there. We are allowing constitutional authority and accountability to be delegated to third parties.

In New York, despite a 20 percent reduction in employees, the payroll is only 1 percent less than it was 2 years ago. Bargaining began last week with the 37,000 bus and subway transit workers, who are demanding wage increases of from 1 to 18 percent. The transit workers union by tradition sets rates for the city's 200,000 clerical and uniform municipal union members. It's easy to see the influence of municipal unions and labor employees on the city, as well as the problems they have caused the city over the years. Furthermore, with union-dominated pension funds holding 35 percent of the city bonds, New York is not likely to make any effort at reform in this area. The unions are buying the city, with taxpayers financing capital improvements and owning a large part of the city debt.

I have tried to give you some specific reasons why collective bargaining and the right to strike should not be extended to public employees. Essentially, my concern is with the disruptive impact that collective bargaining and public-employee strikes have on the democratic government process. I have held public office long enough to respect the idea of accountability of public officials. Maybe it is becoming a rather old-fashioned idea, but I believe that the first place to bring out meaningful change is through the ballot box. Public officials should be prepared to defend their records and be judged on their performance. If labor were granted equal bargaining status in the government bargaining process, this would constitute an unjustifiable surrender of responsibility. To allow public employees to strike would be even more deplorable and cannot be allowed.

With respect to the argument that public employees are badly treated, I would like to say that when I was in Salt Lake City government, employees had a larger wage increase than during any other 7-year period in the history of the city. Secondly, fringe benefits in the public sector are far better than in the private sector. So I think that it is a myth that public employees are badly treated. Witness the long waiting lists to get public-sector jobs. I think the record speaks for itself, and the system has worked well in providing good treatment for government employees. I think the record clearly shows that collective bargaining has done little more than disrupt that process and, in many instances, takes away benefits and flexibility from public employees with ironclad written contracts.

Donald T. Weckstein's Rebuttal

First I would like to say that George Meany does not speak for me any more than I speak for him. President Roosevelt's observation, which Senator Garn cited, is not relevant today in reference to collective bargaining for public employees. The statement was made not as part of any formal policy, but rather in a letter written during 1937 when the impact of strikes on the public welfare was different.

Second, I clearly endorse strong action taken against any striker who engages in violence. However, we are not talking now about violent strikes; we are talking about peaceful strikes. In both the public and private sectors, excesses during strikes must be punished. There are, of course, a great many illegal strikes by public employees, and I think that these strikes are wrong for several reasons, not the least of which is the disrespect for the law they evidence (especially when the strikers are school teachers who are supposed to set an example). If we are going to curtail illegal strikes, we should recognize reality and authorize those strikes which do not interrupt essential services and provide alternatives, such as compulsory arbitration, whenever essential services are involved. In those states which have adopted laws of this kind, the record of labor is fairly good. There are not as many illegal strikes, and the total labor picture is better.

Compulsory arbitration does involve delegation, but such delegation is not at all unusual; government has delegated power in the past. Legislatures delegate all sorts of powers to administrative agencies and sometimes to nongovernment officials as well. The important thing is that this delegation of power should be constrained by adequate guidelines under accepted standards of administrative law. These standards can be spelled out in the statute that authorizes the compulsory arbitration or at the time of delegation. Some states avoid the problem of delegating sovereign power by making the arbitrators public officials while they are engaged in arbitration. Also, a panel of arbitrators can be approved by the legislative body and need not be from out of state.

Another way of limiting discretion of compulsory arbitrators is through final-offer arbitration. Under this device, the arbitrator must chose the final offer of either labor or management. This system encourages both sides to bargain more seriously before arbitration and to make their final offers more reasonable so that they will more likely be accepted by the arbitrator. I would suggest, however, one refinement of this final-offer arbitration system. If the arbitrator finds that neither offer is in the public interest, he should be able to choose the fact finder's recommendation (if fact finding has preceded), or he may reject both offers and ask for new ones.

I believe that individual public employees would like to have the opportunity to decide for themselves whether they will engage in collective bargaining. As in the private sector, they should have an election to decide the issue. Although people are standing in line to get public-sector jobs, they are also standing in line to get private-sector jobs. The question is not whether public employees are receiving enough in salaries and fringe benefits, rather the question is, Is it fair to deny employees a direct voice in decisions concerning economic priorities and the benefits that they receive? Maybe the employees would prefer a reallocation of their earnings with respect to wages and fringe benefits. Is it not fairer and more efficient to allow them to negotiate with their employers through their elected representatives than to follow a paternalistic policy under which good old Mayor Garn will let old Joe, who works in the sanitation department, come in and talk about his problems?

Rightly or wrongly, when intolerable unemployment exists in the private sector, government frequently becomes an employer of the last resort. However, in collective bargaining, when a group seeks wages that exceed productivity, unemployment will result. Some say this outcome does not occur in the public sector, but the fact is that this has happened, for example, in New York, where a 13 percent cut has been made in the number of employees during the fiscal crisis. Again, I point to New York not as a good example of what collective bargaining could do, but as a horror story of what will happen if we do not intelligently engage in collective bargaining. Just as private companies can go bankrupt for bad fiscal policies, so can cities, and New York should be a warning to all cities that they should contain excessive demands on the part of unions.

I think that the fear of bankruptcy will be enough to enforce officials to resist unreasonable demands in public bargaining and your interest and mine will be protected by this fear. However, if public officials do not protect our interests, we can not only vote them out of office, but we can also limit taxation by referendum, as we have done in California. Interestingly, in California a referendum to outlaw the right to strike by public employees did not get enough signatures, but one to limit taxes did.

Jake Garn's Rebuttal

I certainly agree with Dean Weckstein that in 1937 things were a lot different. At that time, municipal employees were treated very poorly. Old employees to whom I have talked have told me so. If a need for union organization was ever demonstrated, it was demonstrated at that time. Therefore, I am rather surprised at Roosevelt's statement that he thought strikes would be disruptive. Workers certainly could not have been treated better in those days than they are today.

On the matter of delegating authority, I believe that a lot of things can be delegated, but that the authority to set the tax rates is not one of those things. The line must be drawn there. A lot of things can be delegated, but when a public official shifts that authority to someone else, accountability is lost. A mayor in Michigan, a good friend of mine, is totally in favor of collective bargaining and binding arbitration. However, he once told me that when he offered an 8 percent raise, the union asked for a 15 percent raise, and the arbitrator gave the union a 22 percent raise. As a result, the mill levy had to be increased by 8 percent. This action was taken by a certified, in-state arbitrator.

Obviously we need to find a balance in the Civil Service. Something that disturbs me so many times about this whole process is that union leaders do things that their rank and file do not want. For example, attempts are being made in Congress to repeal the Hatch Act. The AFL-CIO, the primary instigators, would like to politicize the millions of federally employed workers. They are really pushing to accomplish this goal. Although over 80 percent of the public employees in the Washington area want the protection from political coercion offered by the Hatch Act, George Meany wants to repeal it. Unions are ignoring the rank and file.

Moreover, as I said in my statement, legislatures and Congress impose unionism when the unions cannot win by salesmanship. Unions want compulsion. It is a matter of state right-to-work laws. I favor state right-to-work laws, but I do not favor a national right-to-work law. The other side wants to prohibit states from adopting a right-to-work law to let the people decide.

Again, I agree with Dean Weckstein that we need to return a lot of services to the local level of government, where there is more accountability and more accessibility of elected officials to the people. However, this return just does not happen from a practical standpoint, and the increase in taxes is not forcing it to happen. Too many special interest groups are demanding their piece of the pie, and the level of government centralization and authority of the private sector on the local level of government is increasing. I wish that we could do what Dean Weckstein suggests, but it is a fact that things are going in the other direction.

In Salt Lake City I was not merely "good old Mayor Garn," acting out of the goodness of my heart; I did feel that we should accept a sole bargaining agent for municipal employees. For example, we had a series of meetings over a 3- or 4-month period in the process of determining our budget and what kinds of wage increases we could give. The fire department situation is instructive. This department contained three groups, and I met with the elected representatives of each. In addition, any individual firefighter was welcome to come in and present his views. One year I said, "This is the amount of money that we have for raises." The firefighters responded, "Fine, but we do not like the way it was divided among grades." I replied, "Go ahead and divide it any way you want." Interestingly, the president of the firefighters union (whom I later fired for insubordination) had a plan. He gave the highest raise to first-grade firefighters, and it went down from there. Coincidentally, he was a first-grade firefighter who had taken the promotion exam three times and failed all three. I did not agree with his plan, for I thought that both officers and lower grades were entitled to pay raises, and I did not like the game that they were playing. So I exercised my authority and said no, I am not going to buy your plan.

Another interesting point is that when we have unemployment and a recession, neither occurs in Washington. The big recession of 1974, 1975, and 1976 did not affect Washington because of the stability of public employment. In fact, what usually happens during recessions is that we pass public-service job programs and hire people to work for the government on a temporary basis. Thus government employment generally increases during a recession or high unemployment in the private sector.

Another point to consider closely is that a person can get fired very easily in the private sector. But do you know how hard it is to get fired in the public sector and in Civil Service? It took me 4 years to fire the president of the firefighting union in Salt Lake City—4 years. Although the security in public employment is overwhelmingly an advantage over the private sector, public employees want both that security and collective bargaining. One of the reasons that people line up for government jobs is that that kind of security does not exist in the private sector. They know that they would have to do something really atrocious to be eliminated, particularly on the federal level. I do not agree with President Carter, but when he tries to lessen the number of workers in the public sector, I applaud him.

As a specific example, I mention a fellow who happened to be from Utah. This man had a job that he continued to press Congress to eliminate.

However, he got no satisfaction. He was paid $19,000 by the Department of Health, Education and Welfare; he had nothing to do all day but play classical music records, and he had a secretary who worked for him. After 4 years of pleading and begging, he finally got rid of his job by firing himself.

As for strikes in either the public or private sector, frankly I prefer not to have strikes, but I believe in a worker's legal right to strike. Of course, if I had my druthers, I would rather not see things going as they did with the coal strike. I find the violence just a little bit intolerable.

However, my point is that the line should not be drawn on the basis of who signs the paychecks; rather the line should be based on whether society can tolerate interruption of certain services, and for how long. If a public utilities strike gets to the point at which it threatens the community, it should be enjoined. I should add, however, that when the public utilities are privately owned, such as the telephone companies, and when there is no prohibition against the right to strike by its employees, the companies have had incentive to guard against injury from strikes by automating their functions to a point at which the danger from a strike is not as great as it otherwise would be. Perhaps governments would do the same if they knew strikes were not legal.

Notes

1. Alfred Marshall, *Principles of Economics,* 8th ed. (New York: Macmillan Co., 1920).

2. Albert Rees, *Economics of Trade Unions* (Chicago & London: University of Chicago Press, 1962).

3. Harry Wellington and Ralph Winters, *The Unions and the Cities* (Washington: Brookings Institute, 1971). See also Harry Wellington, "Collective Bargaining in the Public Sector," in B. H. Siegan, *The Interaction of Economics and the Law,* pp. 149–157 (Lexington, Mass.: Lexington Books, D.C. Heath, 1977).

4. Clyde Summers, "Public Employee Bargaining: A Political Perspective," *Yale L.J.* 83 (1974):1156–1200. Summers has collaborated with Harry Wellington on other pieces, but not on the one dealing with public employment.

5. Vegelahn v. Gunter, 167 Mass. 92, 44 N.E. 1077 (1896).

6. ABA Labor Law Section, *Report of Committee on Labor Relations of Government Employees* (1955):89–90.

7. As quoted in Tim Bornstein, "Perspectives on Change in Local Government Collective Bargaining," *Labor L.J.* 28 (1977):431, 444.

8. Since the presentation of this paper, another strike has taken

place—only the second one in the ten years since enactment of the Hawaii statute.

9. Benjamin Aaron, "Reflections on Public Sector Collective Bargaining," *Labor L.J.* 27 (1976):453, 458.

10. Quoted in editorial, *New York Daily News,* November 11, 1974, p. 37. Copyright © 1974, New York News, Inc. Reprinted with permission.

11. Editorial, *The New York Times,* November 10, 1974, sec. 4, p. 14. Copyright © 1974, The New York Times, Inc.

12. Editorial, *The New York Daily News,* November 11, 1974, p. 37. Copyright © 1974, The New York News, Inc. Reprinted with permission.

13. Franklin Delano Roosevelt, letter to Luther C. Steward in *The Public Papers and Addresses of Franklin D. Roosevelt* (1937, "The Constitution Prevails") 325 (New York: Macmillan Co., 1941).

14. Washington Star, August 1, 1974. p. B2.

4

Should Government Controls over Energy Be Limited?

Edward J. Mitchell and
Lee C. White

Edward J. Mitchell's Presentation

My theme can be taken from a statement that one of the young ladies who met me when I arrived in San Diego made. She pointed out that San Diego had just had a power shortage. She described this shortage to me as not being a result of a shortage of energy, but rather as a result of human error. It is my thesis that the energy crisis is entirely the result of human error and has nothing to do with our energy supplies or the lack thereof.

Specifically, the question today is How should we organize the energy market? I do not believe that one can have any appreciation of how to make that choice unless one knows something about the history of the petroleum market in the United States. Unfortunately, descriptions of the horrors of that market do not seem to sound as dramatic as they ought to because people seem to have great difficulty imagining themselves in the petroleum business. I have therefore reconstructed a history of the energy market and its regulation in terms of the entertainment industry.

Imagine that the entertainment industry over the past 50 years has been organized in the same way that the petroleum industry has been—and regulated in the same way. In the 1930s there was a Great Depression and an oversupply of people wanting to enter the entertainment business. This meant unemployment for most actors. Yet some actors, like James Cagney and Humphrey Bogart, were big financial successes. This was judged to be unfair to less popular actors. The government then adopted a set of controls on the production of successful movies. They strictly limited the number of successful movies, thereby leaving a pent up demand for movies that could only be met by unpopular actors and producers. In this way, they kept the incomes of all actors and producers high. This plan worked spectacularly well for the unpopular actors until the 1950s, when foreign movies began to be imported. Foreign movies were cheap and abundant. This threat of foreign-movie competition caused the government to introduce foreign-movie import quotas. Only a small number of foreign movies were allowed into the country each year. The problem was how to determine which movie theaters got to show the foreign movies? It was decided that the foreign movies would only be shown in very small Midwestern theaters. The reason being that those theaters were extremely uneconomical and would otherwise have gone out of business. The problem with that solution was that people in the Midwest did not like foreign movies, so the Midwestern movie theaters sold the movies back to the Eastern movies theaters.

In 1960, attention turned to recording artists; it was decided that a different price would be charged for each individual record, but since there were millions of different records, this bureaucratic process of regulation broke down. So it was decided that the price of records would be set depending on the region in which the recording artist was born. The country was divided into six regions. Because the price was set so low, some recording artists decided that they could make more money as truck drivers. The supply of recordings then fell, and there were not enough to go around. There was a peculiarity of the law, that recordings made and sold in the same state were not subject to price controls; thus there was a boom in record sales in those states where good singers happened to be born. People who liked good music had to move to states where good singers were born. It was also decided that old singers, having been trained in a period when the training costs were low, should get lower wages than new singers. Also, it was realized that if we paid old singers low wages, they would not leave the singing profession, because they had already been in it for 20 years, and would probably stick it out. It was still assumed that young singers would be stupid enough to enter the industry at the high wages, even knowing as they did that when they became old, their wages would not keep up with those of young singers.

After the price controls of records, we then obtained price controls on the movies themselves, and as a result, many movie producers and actors moved abroad. In order to make up for the shortage of movies at home, we began importing foreign movies in enormous quantities, most of which were made by American actors and American producers abroad. Foreign governments saw the enormous opportunity to milk this demand abroad and put tremendous export taxes on movies. Prices of movies in the United States soared, while the price of American movies remained under control. People blamed American movie producers and actors for the high prices. With the foreign prices soaring beyond the control of our government, price controls were extended to theaters, and movies were allocated among the theaters. The government based its estimate of movie demand on poor data. We therefore had movie theaters open 24 hours a day in Michigan, trying to attract customers, while at the same time New Jersey people waited in line 6 hours in order to go to the movies.

With low controlled prices for domestic movies, there were fewer around, and all the theaters wanted them. The government decided to give the cheap American movies to theaters that seated less than ten people because they were uneconomical. So great was the government subsidy to small theaters that you could build a new small theater and the government would return your total investment back in the form of subsidies in 7 months.

In 1977, a new President came in who announced a program that would solve the problem of high prices and little entertainment. His solution was to tell Americans to stop going to the movies and to stop listening to records. In the long term, he promised new and cleaner forms of entertainment that would cost three to ten times as much as current entertainment. This, he said, would prevent consumers from being ripped off by conventional movie producers and recording artists.

Some professors then took an advertisement in the *Washington Post,* arguing that our entertainment policy resulted in artificially high prices, unemployed American actors and singers, far more foreign movies than Americans really wanted to see, enormous profits for foreign governments, the continued use and building of miniscule theaters, and looking down the road, the prospect of scandalously expensive forms of entertainment that people might pay for simply because there was nothing else available. The professors' solution was simply to let anybody entertain who wanted to, and let anyone pay for it as they saw fit. They claimed that if the government simply stepped aside, the crisis would sort itself out. Journalists, lawyers, and politicians were especially hostile to this idea, calling it "naive" and "a weak response to a serious national challenge." They said it would result in large incomes for successful entertainers, and most of these entertainers came from just one or two places, neither of which was New York or Washington.

Of course, the entertainment policies and programs that I have just described are silly. No one looking at the entertainment business today would argue that we would have been well served had we chosen these policies. Yet, if you simply replace movies with oil, records with natural gas, and theaters with refineries, the foregoing is a precise, although superficial glimpse of the history of the U.S. petroleum industry over the past half century under federal and state regulation. It is superficial because no short description could do justice to the imagination exercised by federal bureaucrats. The themes of petroleum regulation over the past generation are first, maximize the cost of producing energy by subsidizing unsuccessful enterprises, resources, and technology and discouraging efficient ones, and second, offer selected groups of consumers cheaper forms of energy, while forcing other consumers to pay far more than is necessary.

It is important to stress that all these policies, programs, and plans were carefully thought out and debated. There are volumes of congressional testimony and executive studies to back up all the decisions. All interest groups and ideologies were represented. These programs were enacted under Democratic and Republican, conservative and liberal governments. All were responding to public pressures and public opinion. All the agencies involved were accountable to the public. Their purposes, the rationales for these programs, varied from conservation to national security to consumer protection. There was one common element in all these plans: the public would be better served by government control than by the market.

Now let me concede that obviously there are certain proper government interventions that could improve the petroleum market. We must control, for example, environmental damage; we must deal with OPEC as a monopoly; we must prepare for foreign supply interruptions. All these are legitimate functions of government that cannot be carried out efficiently in the private sector. What we must guard against are government controls that are used to further special interests or naive ideologies. In the past, the effects of these interests and these ideologies have been devastating to our standard of living; they have created shortages, and they have unnecessarily raised the costs of energy. I think we all appreciate the role of special interests in formulating government policy. I think what is less appreciated is the extent to which special interests have declined in importance and philosophies or ideologies have ascended.

The oil industry has been a spectacularly successful lobby for most of the history that I have related, but since the mid 1960s, the influence of large oil companies has plummeted. If you measure power by the legislation that is passed in your favor, the oil industry was one of the most powerful segments of our society for a number of decades. But by that same measure, the oil industry must be one of the weaker elements of our society today, because the very favorable legislation that they passed in earlier decades has been removed in recent decades. The depletion allowance and import quotas are gone, and in their place are government controls on oil and gas prices that reduce them to a fraction of their competitive free-market level. It would be hard to find an industry that suffered more punitive legislation in the past decade than the oil industry (I would explicitly exclude the small oil producers and refiners).

Unfortunately, the passage of influence from producers to consumers has not resulted in an energy policy favorable to consumers. This is so because there are no organized consumer interests, except in those cases where the consumers are industrial firms. There are only politicians with liberal voting records that claim to favor consumers and the so-called consumerists. However, I believe that a liberal voting record and the cry of consumerism is ideology and not in fact real representation of consumer interests.

Let me take one case from the energy field: the regulation of natural gas prices. Low ceiling prices unquestionably mean cheaper gas for some people, including myself (I am from southern Michigan, which has greatly benefited by cheap natural gas, held down by federal price controls). But most Americans do not heat with gas anymore. We use oil or electricity. The reason that this is so is that low federal prices have held down the production of gas in this country and have forced a number of people to use oil and electricity. This additional demand for oil and electricity has pushed up oil and electricity prices and is indeed an important factor in the development of the OPEC cartel. Thus users of oil and electricity are worse off since they outnumber users of gas, and there are more consumers worse off by gas price controls than better off. And yet, gas price controls are still considered by consumer groups to favor consumers. As a result of relying on what is in essence an ideological response, many politicians from New England for example, continually reject natural gas deregulation, while no group in the country would be more obviously benefited by deregulation. The sophisticated people from that area are well aware of that. New England congressmen are not alone; voting on energy bills in the House of Representatives is overwhelmingly along ideological lines. We are no longer talking about special interests in energy politics. I can predict the outcome of 80 to 90 percent of the votes on all energy bills, just by knowing a congressman's ADA and ACA rating, his rating by the Consumer Federation of America, whether he is a Democrat or a Republican, or from a producing or consuming state.

In spite of the shortages, the long lines at gas stations, and the sudden price increases, which I believe have been induced by government planning, there is still a fear among citizens that the petroleum industry is a monopoly and therefore must be controlled by the government. There are a number of tests of monopoly, the most common test being the question of whether high profits have existed in the industry for a long period of time. In the case of the petroleum industry, a number of studies have been done, including at least one of my own, and all have concluded that over the past two or three decades, the profits of petroleum companies have been normal, whether you measure them by the accounting data or realized gains by stockholders in the forms of dividends and stock price appreciation.

Actually, it does not matter much what the profits of the oil companies are as far as the consumer is concerned. They are such a small percentage of the cost of petroleum that it does not matter much whether the petroleum industry is a philanthropy, or whether the petroleum industry is a monopoly. For example, in 1974, a dynamite year for oil profits and the occasion of the alleged rip-off of the consumer, accounting profits for a gallon of gasoline were just over 2 cents. This was their big year, remember? Cash payments to the stockholders by the fifteen largest companies averaged just over ½ cent per gallon. Had stockholders of all these companies agreed to convert them into philanthropies, to donate their dividends to consumers, and had consumer prices fallen by that amount, the reduction in prices to consumers would have been one-twentieth the level of gasoline excise taxes and one-fifteenth the margin earned by independent retail dealers. Indeed, it would have been entirely offset by a small uptick in state excise taxes in that year.

I do not want to leave you with the idea, however, that the profits of the petroleum companies are irrelevant. If oil companies operated as philanthropies, oil prices would certainly rise, since profit is the only force in the world that reduces costs. To maximize profits, you have to minimize costs. Politicians and bureaucrats who are, after all, the only substitutes we have in this world for private businessmen are not interested in minimizing costs. They are interested in maximizing their own status and influence. Maximizing status and influence means maximizing budgets, which is the same as maximizing costs.

It also has been alleged that oil companies engage in all sorts of peculiar behavior, such as vertical integration, exchange agreements, and joint ventures. I should tell you that many other industries engage in precisely the same thing, and statistics show that most other industries are more vertically integrated than the petroleum industry. There are at least two explanations for oil company behavior. One is consistent with competition, and the other, with collusion. If these two concepts mean anything, then empirical tests can be designed to determine whether behavior is actually competitive or collusive. This involves the application of the social science of economics to the case at hand. I would like to know where the scientific studies of the petroleum market show that the industry is monopolistic are? In a recent poll, more than 75 percent of the professors specializing in the petroleum industry regulation field expressed the view that the petroleum industry was not monopolistic at any level of operation, whether producing, refining, transporting, or marketing. Interestingly enough, there are areas of the energy industry where many professional economists do find evidence of monopoly, but not in oil. And there are no studies to the contrary. I believe that oil is attacked mainly because it is more visible and because of the folklore of our country that casts oil as monopolistic.

Another criticism of the market as an institution in dealing with the energy problem is that even if it is more efficient, it is not equitable. The accusation is that the market lacks a sense of justice. It is difficult to argue against that criticism because justice, many of us would believe, is not uniquely determined by human reason. I suppose there are as many justices as there are theologies, and the market's sense of justice may not correspond with your own. This criticism of the market and my research of what goes into the market controlled by government has led me to the following empirical definitions: the market is an institution that creates affluence and distributes it unevenly. The government is an institution that creates poverty and distributes it "fairly." Obviously, the word *fairly* is in quotes because fair means whatever the outcome of the political process provides. Fair means that I get cheap natural gas in southern Michigan, while people in North Carolina, New Jersey, and Vermont go broke trying to meet fuel bills.

To return to the entertainment industry, why is it fair that someone earns a fortune because he was born with flexible hips and durable vocal chords? To my mind, most people do not chastise others for the peculiar tastes that give rise to these fortunes. We accept the market outcome, and we fuss very little about its equity. Why do we place such an emphasis on political justice in petroleum, but not in amusement? I think that when we decide to allow petroleum companies and consumers the same rights we grant to rock musicians and their audiences, we will find the public much better served.

Lee C. White's Presentation

The question presented by this debate is very important in resolving whether we are going to have a capitalistic system, a socialistic system, or what we truly had over the past decades, namely, a mixture, or a pluralistic system. So far as I am concerned, my background, my prejudices, and my biases all go in an opposite direction. It is not that I do not have faith in the market-place; I do. There are numerous illustrations of where the marketplace not only runs relatively well, but is perceived by people in this country to run well.

I have not really thought through the entertainment analogy that Professor Mitchell has given us; my own feeling is that it does not work well. The one I would like to use is the citrus crop. We all know that if there is an early frost, we do not have as many oranges as we otherwise would. Expecting the demand to be relatively level, a frost is going to push the price very high. Since demand remains the same, but supply falls, it will cost more money for oranges. We have a choice when that happens; if we are wealthy enough and are willing to pay more, we can have orange juice. But some people will not be able to afford orange juice and will have to drink tomato juice instead. There is, in short, some elasticity; we have the freedom to decide how much orange juice we want to consume, and that is true with a lot of commodities. It is, I submit, much less true of energy. It is, of course, possible for some people not to drive to work, but not with the *present* underdevelopment of mass transportation in some areas (especially the West Coast).

In 1971 President Nixon decided to impose wages and price controls. It was very harsh medicine, but it was deemed to be the right thing to do by him, and I dare say that over the period of time, as we look back, we realize that it was not perfect, but it seemed to do the trick. It did not last long, and that is one of the benefits of it. And so Congress removed the federal authority to control wages and prices in general. Yet there was one exception; oil prices. There, public opinion polls were all the congressmen had to guide them on the people's sentiments. So I take comfort in knowing that we as a nation realized that energy is different. Those of us who live in colder parts of the country may be able to turn our thermostats down to 65°, but not much below that. We may be able to increase our home insulation, and I hope we do, but we can go only so far. We need energy as much as we need any other commodity. So I personally have very little difficulty with the notion that it is legitimate to impose controls on energy prices. I know the horror stories about natural gas controls; at one point in my life, I earned my living setting natural gas rates. But at the risk of appearing unduly modest, I do not think that federal regulators can claim all the credit for our gas shortages.

I would like now to spend a little bit of time on natural gas regulation in the past and (to the extent I can) the future. The reason why I equivocate is that this week there is a movement finally to solve this complex problem of gas regulation, which has been with us (in the Congress) since the 1940s. We have only to go back 10 minutes to the subject of the artificial balance in supply and demand in natural gas. But there are 40 million families (at four persons per family, that's 160 million people) who are hooked up to natural gas (and my family is one of them) and who do not have the freedom to switch to coal or oil. Even a switch to electricity is very impractical for most of us. Therefore, there can be no dispute that we need to regulate the gas company that sells us our gas and control the price of transporting the gas between producing areas and consuming areas. What the dispute centers around is Should the people who produce natural gas be able to sell it to the pipelines at whatever is the going rate? During my tenure at the Federal Power Commission (FPC), the method used for determining the rates that would be fixed for natural gas was conceptually rather simple: the average cost of producing gas was determined through lengthy hearings, and then some additional money was included for noncost items; then the Commission, in calculating the allowed rate, included a return on investment of 15 to 18 percent. This method had been used before I became a part of the FPC, and it has been used since. I submit that it is not unfair. What I propose is that Congress put this system into law—that 18 percent be the allowable profit. I have put this proposition in vain to people from the gas industry (basically the petroleum industry encompasses both oil and natural gas—85 percent of our natural gas is produced by the same companies who produce 85 to 90 percent of our oil). So you see, the natural gas industry is not made up of a bunch of wildcatters from Texas. The major oil and gas producers tell me that they do not separate their returns on oil and natural gas. Rather, they say that they are integrated companies.

This week we have a new dispute in Washington; Congress created the Energy Department and the Energy Information Administration. The question is, What is the Energy Department going to do with the data submitted to it? Secretary Schlesinger tells us that we have some problems with the proprietary nature and confidentiality of this information. It seems that a decision is about to be made that this information cannot even be forwarded to the Justice Department.

What it comes down to is that we need protection on energy; we cannot just leave energy prices to the marketplace, because there really is no marketplace. Let me tell you two different things that concern me. First is the artificiality of "our oil market." Our oil price is now roughly pegged at the world oil price insofar as the congressional debate is concerned. The President says, "Let's put our domestic price at the world price in terms of what it should be today by imposing an 'equalization tax' on cheaper to produce domestic oil to lift the price to the world price" (representing some $40 billion in new taxes over a 3-year period). The industry says, "Let the world price fix the price because we need to make the money necessary to find new oil supplies, and we should sell oil at the replacement cost." Yet, what disturbs me is that the world price came from the fourteen oil ministers from the Organization of Petroleum Exporting Countries (OPEC) sitting around and deciding a price that has nothing to do with the cost of finding oil, but rather with their ability to control the supply of oil. With all the problems of federal price setting for natural gas in the last 20 years, it turns out that Texas has a gas surplus. The Texas Railroad Commission (which determines the rate at which gas and oil can be produced in Texas) decided recently to cut back the production of gas because of a softening in the price. If the price can be held up by somebody with control, I would rather have the imperfect bureaucrats do it (at just and reasonable levels, as the law requires). If you know of any natural gas companies that have gone bankrupt, please tell me. I know there is great uncertainty because we do not know what our nation's pricing policies with respect to gas will be; I can understand the reluctance of people who are going to make a major investment to move ahead until they understand the ground rules. I would be uneasy myself if I were president of Gulf Oil. But once the policy is formulated, it is my thesis that people who will be able to make 16 to 35 percent on their investments will do so.

Even though this is beyond the ambit of the debate, there is an awful lot of oil and natural gas to be discovered on public lands, the bulk of it offshore. I believe it would make a great deal of sense for the government (who owns that property in trust for all Americans) to develop these resources itself rather than sell it to the highest bidder. Indeed, we are the only industrialized nation in the world that leaves the pursuit of oil and natural gas to corporations whose sole motivation is profit. Now there is nothing wrong with profit, but there are other considerations present here; one is stockpiling. Being an alumnus of the Tennessee Valley Authority (TVA), I believe that TVA engineers are just as good as the engineers that work for private companies, and I believe that government technology can do just as good a job as private technology. After all, an electron going through a wire does not know whether it was sent there by the local utility company or by the TVA. This would also give the government some idea as to what it is like to run an energy company. Also, the expertise it would give the government would ameliorate the lack of knowledge and information that the government presently has.

Edward J. Mitchell's Rebuttal

I am pleased that Mr. White chose natural gas as his example to show how energy works. He indicated the procedure for determining prices for natural gas: you find out what it costs to produce natural gas, then set the price giving the producer a very handsome rate of return at 18 percent. But let me mention a few things about the world of natural gas.

There is, on the one hand, natural gas, which costs essentially nothing. That is, oil may be discovered that has natural gas mixed in with it, or natural gas may have been discovered a long time ago in a well that is already operational. On the other hand, there is gas that has to be explored to be found. So since you have "free" natural gas and "expensive" natural gas, how is the cost of finding natural gas determined? Which gas is used? The only gas the FPC uses is the already discovered gas, the "free" gas. If the price of gas is 25 cents per cubic foot, who in his right mind is going to go out and discover gas that will cost $1 per cubic foot? Whenever you observe the historic costs of natural gas, you are observing a particular segment of the market. I cannot think of anything less relevant to what the price of gas should be. The price of gas today should be high enough to induce the producer to produce it and low enough to induce the buyer to buy it. If it gets too expensive, no one would want it, and therefore no one would produce it. In other words, set the rate by the law of supply and demand. If gas were priced that way, the rate of return would not be 18 percent, but much lower.

After taxes, 18 percent is a very high rate of return. If you look at pure oil and gas producing companies over the last 20 years, you will not find many that really earn 18 percent after taxes. The depletion rates are gone, and the tax rates for the oil companies are right there with the other corporations. Look at stock dividends—very few are at 18 percent per year. What I am suggesting is that if you used the market, you would get more gas and a lower rate of profit.

Mr. White says that he is concerned with high oil prices, and that OPEC is the source of those high prices. I am concerned with high oil prices too, but the only source of competition in this country to OPEC is the oil and gas producers, and they are the very ones being penalized by regulation. We offer our producers a fraction of the prices we offer to a foreign cartel. Not only do we not compete with the cartel, but we subsidize them by holding down our prices to pay whatever they ask. Mr. White asks me how many oil companies I know of that have gone bankrupt. I have not counted, but now there are some 2,000 fewer producing companies than there were when he entered the FPC. Now I do not think that they all went out of business because they made so much money that they could retire. Between 1959 and 1971, the number of drilling rigs looking for oil fell by 50 percent, and it still has not reached the 1959 level. I think the statistics clearly show that during the period after Mr. White came in, the incentive to produce gas fell substantially and companies did leave the business.

I do not believe that Congress should guarantee the energy companies a rate of return or escalating prices. The market should guarantee that. If we deregulated gas and the price did not go up as fast as inflation, it would be great for the consumers but unfortunate for the energy companies. When you adopt a market as the ultimate price setter, you take the good with the bad. If deregulation gives us much more gas than is demanded, the market will drive the price of gas down. If that happens—if the gas companies lose money—fine. They take the gamble, so it is their risk. The regulatory approach works both ways; it very often holds the price down, but more often than most people are aware (especially in fields such as airlines, trucking, and railroads), it raises the price, aiding the producer at the expense of the consumer. And I am concerned about the consumer movement. It seems to have chosen a road tied too closely with government control against its natural ally, the market. I think this is very unfortunate for the organized consumer movement.

With regard to how regulation works, former FPC chairman Richard Dunn gave a talk to my class in Michigan just after he left the Commission. He was the one who raised prices from 50 cents to $1.40 per thousand cubic feet of natural gas. The FPC went through an enormous amount of time taking testimony on pricing; Mr. Dunn took all this testimony to the lawyers and told them to give him the lowest and highest allowable prices based on the studies. That range was between 40 cents and $2.40. He chose $1.40 because he thought that price would stave off some of the bills of impeachment pending against him in Congress. Thus the price set is politically determined. This is not a particularly good way for society to decide what the price of natural gas should be.

OPEC was created in 1960, and prices soared for the first time in 1973. I contend that prices soared not because of OPEC, but because of domestic controls. Between 1960 and 1969 (the first 9 years of OPEC), the world price of oil fell substantially. It is not OPEC itself that is responsible for higher oil prices, but rather a fundamental shift in the supply and demand of the world.

The United States plays a large role in changing the world's supply and demand. When we adopted the policy of keeping oil prices low and reserves low, we had to import, and then OPEC raised prices. This was my movie hypothetical. The Arabs were just delighted to have Americans go over there, produce oil, and sell it for many times more than it sold for in the United States. In fact, we subsidize the cartel. Consider the State Department policy: not only has the State Department been in favor of the OPEC cartel, but it has been in favor of even higher prices than those set by OPEC. The position of our government is to give OPEC what it wants, to encourage higher prices for oil. I do not think that is in our national interest, but it is our national policy.

There is some evidence that increases in prices keep consumption down. Europeans have had much higher prices for gasoline than we have—they have not had the price controls we have—yet they consume less oil than we do. And in the United States the evidence shows that there is reduced consumption to the extent that the oil prices have gone up. But price increases in the United States have been basically caused by inflation, with the "real" price of oil remaining constant. Thus we should not expect decreases in consumption in the United States, because there has been no real rise in oil prices. This is why, during the embargo, other parts of the world did not have the problems of long lines at the gas stations. Lines were unique to the United States because we had a Federal Energy Office that allocated resources during the embargo. In northern Michigan there were gas stations staying open 24 hours a day because they had to get rid of gasoline with new shipments coming in. That was not the fault of the petroleum companies; it was the fault of the Energy Office. That office allocated gasoline during the crisis on the basis of data that were 2 years old instead of allowing the market to decide where the gasoline should go. While people in New Jersey had to wait in long lines to get gasoline, there were no lines at all in Ann Arbor, Michigan—and this is called regulation.

To use a California example, there is oil off Long Beach selling for $4 per barrel, while OPEC oil is $14 per barrel. Producers warn us of a possibility of massive shut-ins because it is not economical to produce oil in the United States. Now I am not interested in getting prices of gasoline up in the United States for their own sake, but I am interested in getting prices up in this country for the sake of doing something about the OPEC cartel. It is one thing to pay an American oil producer a reasonable price to cover costs and another thing to pay an OPEC producer one-hundred times his costs. Whether in the long run we will get the prices of oil down, I cannot say, but we have to get our price up to the OPEC price to begin with. If we reduce our demand for imports, perhaps the price of world oil will fall. At least it will not rise as fast as it would otherwise. No one can predict the true price of oil, but I can predict one thing: the price of oil will be higher if we have an oil industry that is not allowed to compete fairly with foreign oil producers.

Lee C. White's Rebuttal

Professor Mitchell reminds me that there are those who think that during the time when I was with the Federal Power Commission the genesis for the shortage was created. I have to tell the truth: so far as I know, the one other person who believes that is my mother (and she is very proud of me—she cannot believe that her little boy is responsible for all that). Yet in 1965, when the price was first set for drilling in the Permian Basin, drillings increased there. The fixed price was then 18 cents per thousand cubic feet, and we are now up to $1.40 and rising. What really contributed in large measure to this was our discovery of the existence of very serious air pollution problems in 1968. In 1968, for the first time, we consumed more natural gas than we produced. For example, in the Los Angeles area, it was forbidden to burn gas with sulfur in it, so natural gas was pushed to the forefront. The same thing happened in St. Louis and New York. So in 1968, consumption of natural gas doubled. As I have said before, I can understand the reluctance of people today to invest in natural gas production so long as the regulation issue is still unresolved by Congress. I do not believe that there is anything essentially wonderful about regulation, but however bad it is, it would be worse now to let the controls off in the short term (I do not know about the long term). But in the short term we must prevent exploitation by those who have the power to exploit us. Right now, I do not think the free market can do this.

I would allow controls for inflation. In fact, all the proposals now before Congress do take inflation into account. Indexing is perfectly acceptable now, and I do not know of any consumer groups that oppose it.

To clarify an earlier point, the 15 to 18 percent profit that the energy companies make is *after* taxes on invested capital. One of the costs of producing natural gas is the amount of taxes paid by the producer. With our present tax structure, many of our petroleum companies do not pay a great deal of taxes. But these taxes are a part of the cost of producing gas. So you see, the present system is not at all unfair to producers. As far as the 2,000 to 3,000 producers who are not there anymore, most were swallowed up by the others. Those remaining are different kinds of groups. In fact, new producers do not just go out on their own and start drilling; they work out arrangements with the existing companies. Most of our existing reserves are in the hands of a very few large companies, and many producers do not want to work with the existing companies.

So you see, sometimes the arguments that we use are a little bit off the mark, those by both Professor Mitchell and myself. Professor Mitchell honestly believes that the market place works, and I do not—especially when we have so many other factors. Look at the depletion allowance, for example. The question that someone should have asked is, If you look at things in the short term, you will hold down prices today, but there will be no gas left for our children and grandchildren. Should we not leave some for them? In the real world, there is a tendency to want to live for today and think technology will produce other techniques for the future. But can we be that callous about our children and grandchildren? Do not forget that this issue of providing energy for the future is one of the many issues we have to grapple with when we decide who shall set our national policy.

Let me tell you some of the processes that we went through when I was chairman of the FPC. The most prolific area in the country for natural gas is south Louisiana, on the coast just off Louisiana. Roughly one-third of the natural gas that moves in commerce in this country comes from that area. We were down there trying to determine the cost of producing natural gas when a fellow came to see me from the pipeline industry. He asked me if the FPC was willing to let the producers and distributors of gas work out their own arrangement. I answered that the FPC was not going to bind itself in advance to any such arrangement in an area where one-third of our natural gas comes from, but we would listen to them.

Using the good offices of the FPC, the producers and distributors each sent a team, and they came up with a price, by some concensus, of 20 cents per cubic foot. Now the Commission had this recommendation, and the hearing officer came up with a different recommendation. The result we came up with was 19½ cents—very close to what they wanted. In fact, one of the members of the Commission said, "Let's give them what they want. This way they will not blame us." In fact, a few years later, under a different administration, the price was set at 26 cents, exactly what the producers and distributors wanted. Those were the days when we were talking about pennies and nickels, not quarters and half-dollars. The producers, when they signed this, said 26 cents was all they would need for 5 years. Would you believe that within 2 years they came back and asked for more? But the distributors later gave up on it. So maybe in a funny sort of way the market did work, because this certainly was not anything the producers were up to.

Right now the President has proposed a price of $1.75, and Senator Jackson is proposing $1.84. In the gas industry, while you mention most things in terms of pennies and nickels, it is multiplied by trillions of cubic feet, and each penny of increase raises the price of the discovered reserves by $200 million. These are very large sums. Do not forget that poor people pay a much higher percentage of their budgets for energy than do wealthy people. This is another consideration that must be given weight. I suppose there is never a good time to make a good change, and that is why we should continue to regulate this industry.

The OPEC cartel signifies the energy problem in a dramatic fashion. Shortages are also a problem. It is very hard to worry about things a decade in advance. We are talking about a finite resource—there is only so much oil and gas out there. Surely the economic incentive can be changed to determine how much of it is deliverable. In the early 1980s, according to the Department of Energy, we are going to start to go downhill with respect to discoveries of oil and gas. Already we are trying to turn coal to gas to electricity all in one process. While there are problems with coal, we will get to the point where we are going to have to make some shifts. The President has got to try to get us to conserve energy, and his policy is to get us to use less by increasing the price. Economists tell us to increase the price and the demand will drop off. But look at the gasoline consumption since the 1973 embargo. We are consuming more energy at a higher price. So there is some doubt about the responsiveness of demand to price. The President is trying to get us to insulate our homes, and the automobile industry is now mandated to produce automobiles that will get more miles to the gallon. I approve of these methods, but I would go further; I would limit imports from abroad to lessen the supply and make people conserve. We did that when we were trying to keep the price of oil up from 1959 until the Nixon administration. At that time, the world oil price was below the domestic price. We kept out the cheap stuff to encourage our domestic industry. This cost the consumer 85 billion more dollars. I would favor going back to that approach to break up OPEC.

We almost slipped one by OPEC in the dark of night. When Congress was working on Department of Energy legislation (with a different committee than usually works on energy issues), Congressman Conyers of Detroit came up with the idea of having the federal government buy up all the imported oil and bring it over here. It made so much sense that it was approved. The next day they had another vote, and it lost. In this sort of thing, it is difficult to understand what is the effect and what is the cause. It is like what we called the "Queen Mary syndrome" in law school. The Queen Mary syndrome is when a fellow comes home and says to his wife, "I was at the pier today. I leaned against the Queen Mary and she went out to sea." Even though there were three tugs pushing the ship, he could still honestly say that he leaned against the Queen Mary and it went out to sea. Now OPEC had a lot of reasons for coming into being, but I think we perhaps could have undertaken a stronger effort to prevent its birth.

Energy is different from other things in regard to the law of supply and demand, because energy is not a commodity that presents much opportunity for reduction. I am perfectly willing to admit that on the supply side, we have to adopt effective policies, but I am not accepting the notion that the only way to increase supply is to take off the controls. People are making money today, and as far as I am concerned, if I were in the business, I would like to have a greater incentive too. However, the incentive is already adequate—if you take off the controls, you are going to add from a thousand to infinity and give a windfall, if my theory is accurate. In an average year, it is only possible to decrease your energy consumption by so much.

I have been asked how I can rely so heavily on government regulation, considering that the price of gasoline has gone up only five times what it was in the same period of time that postage rates rose by ten times what they were. The syllogism is, Why should the government be given responsibility for anything else after they so totally ruined this? With respect to government inefficiency in the Postal Service, yes, the Post Office may be inept. But with respect to energy, my experience has been with the Tennessee Valley Authority (TVA). Their personnel is as good as any privately held power company, and I do not think that who you work for makes a difference as to the quality of your work. Look at public television, for example.

I am not advocating a socialized energy policy—I know the experiences of England—but it has been my experience that if government does an effective job, things are not too bad. Most people agree with me regarding the effectiveness of the TVA. While it is true that some government agencies are grossly inefficient, this is not the case with the TVA. Look at Comsat, for example. In order to maintain a communications satellite system, we need equipment that is exclusively for use in national defense systems (if we agree that government should be involved in matters of national defense). We had a dilemma, since communications are generally run by the private sector. So Comsat, a hybrid, came into being, and it has worked out rather well. We also have a reasonably efficient public radio and television network and a number of municipally owned electrical companies that operate about as well as the private ones. So I really do not think that there is any monopoly on bureaucratic stupidity, whether it is inside or outside the government. Amtrak is a perfect example. Amtrak came into being only when many private railroads went right down the tube.

Reasonable people do differ as to what is best for the consumer. Some believe that the free market is the best way for the consumer to get what he wants. Based on my background and experience, I do not have enough confidence and trust in the petroleum industry in the year 1978 to place myself in its hands totally for my energy needs. I am not that frightened by the prospect of imperfect government regulation set up to help people. I do not think that all our problems can be traced to the government. It took some pretty horrible experiences to get antitrust laws and other such regulation into being, and these were all responses to abuses by the business community. Today we have environmental protection—do you truly believe that we would have gone forward with the progress we have made on air and water quality without federal direction? Such concerns cannot be left to business and other profit-making entities. Could a corporation accountable to its shareholders justify making a lower profit because it had to put in equipment that would reduce air pollution? Of course not. Consumers need a little protection from a market that is less than perfect. I do not hold that consumers are best served all the time by government controls. Here we are talking about energy, and I am able to make a distinction. On trucking, I have a different view. I do not think logical consistency requires us to proceed all one way or all another way. Consumer groups did not complain when Congress took off the price controls that Nixon put on. Happily, in my view, an exception was made for energy. That is what we are talking about: doing things that have to be done.

For 50 years the government held the Naval Petroleum Reserve, which was to go to national defense. I do not think that the government should take over private corporations, but if we could create a reserve for our national defense security, why not for our national economic security? There are some times when it is good for people to do things other than for a profit motive. I do not have any basic objection to profits. But I also recognize that some legitimate activities must be undertaken by government.

5 Should Government Deregulation Be Coupled with Deconcentration of Industry?

Gary Hart and *Harold Demsetz*

Gary Hart's Presentation

I intend to base my argument almost exclusively on public policy. And in that connection, let me just say that the founding fathers (in my judgment of history) were concerned, among other things, with the consequences of the concentration of power in the United States, not only in their own time, but on into the future. To guard against that they established in our government a system of checks and balances. That system was designed to preserve a separation of power between different branches of government and, secondarily, a dispersion of power and final authority among the citizenry. The principle of decentralized decision making was also applied in shaping the economy. Competition and the free market were viewed not only as instruments for achieving material purposes and progress, but also as a means to achieve social values, to promote the value of individual initiative and limited government, and to guard against the use of private power to the detriment of public interest. Abuses in authority in our recent history underscore the importance of decentralized decision making within that framework of checks and balances. Even in this day and age, our founding fathers cannot be dismissed as anachronistic philosophers. Their focus was what our focus should be today.

The issue is not so much the economy, big or small, integrated or not, but rather it is what kind of economic structure is most likely to result in the kind of society that we want. Granted, our economy has changed drastically since the days of the Revolution, and it is no longer just based on creativity and risk of failure. It is also geared to predictability and the problem of stability. I do not argue this point. The industrial revolution and the population explosion overturned America's village economy. Among other factors, in its place, we now have a marriage of private interests and government protection. It has come to be known, instead of free enterprise, as private enterprise.

Free enterprise, as usually presumed and described in the early days of this country, could soon be going the way of the dinosaur. I think one of the greatest threats to genuine free enterprise is government intervention in the private sector. In the name of consumer protection, there are more and more demands for restricting the freedom of firms to set their own prices and types of services. In the name of job protection, there are calls for restriction on international free trade. In the name of economic stability, there are more and more subsidies and so-called incentives to private business. But there is another, more serious threat to free enterprise. This is the increasing concentration of economic power. It seems that virtually all our economy, outside of the small service businesses, is drifting into either large-scale multinational conglomerates or modern style grids. It is this trend toward conglomeration that I think is very disturbing. Combining not only the processes of fabrication, but also economic control and what I would consider to be anti-Jeffersonian political power. The statistics are particularly striking, I think, in the manufacturing sector. By the end of 1974, the top 200 corporations listed in *Fortune Magazine's* top 500, comprising less than one-tenth of 1 percent of all U.S. manufacturing firms, account for two-thirds of the manufacturing assets, and three-fifths of the sales, employment, and net income after taxes. The statistics also reveal that these same 200 firms now control what the top 500 controlled 25 years ago, in gross numbers. Experts estimate that by sometime in the 1980s, the top 200 firms of that day will control roughly three-fourths of all U.S. manufacturing assets, about the same share as is held by the top 500 today. The issue is not statistics on aggregate concentration; rather, it is the potential that some firms have to condition and shape national economic policy. The fact is that increasingly, fewer and fewer people are making decisions that have the greatest impact on the economy. Our most basic industries are among the ones most highly concentrated.

Government bail-outs of Lockheed and Penn Central indicate that already some firms have become, in the minds of some, "too big to lose." The danger is that, at some point, an interlocking group of certain men and women will end up with the controlling shares in American business. The result would be that a few bad decisions by a relatively small group will have a disasterous impact on the health and future of our economy. Now I believe very strongly that our nation is at the crossroads of an economic evolution. We can continue along what I think is our present course toward increasing corporate power and the related increase in the power of labor unions and regulatory authority, or I think we can make our economic system more compatible with our traditional political values of individual initiative and limited government. Such a course would promote more competition wherever it would work in the best interests of the American public. Now I am not advocating a return to the "Mom and Pop" stores of early Americana, and I am not saying that big is bad and small is beautiful. The fact is that some things require large-scale production for optimum efficiency.

I think it is important that the unit of efficiency in many industries is the plant, and not the firm or corporation. But it is also important to remember that there comes a point of diminishing returns. I mean this not only in the classical economic sense, where at a certain point profits diminish in proportion to additional investment. There also can be diminishing returns of other kinds; a lack of innovation, a lack of responsiveness to changing consumer needs, and a lack of sensitivity to the quality of life in the community. Small firms swallowed up by large conglomerates often lose the entrepreneurial spirit in the process. Local plant managers are separated from corporate executives. Corporate executives are often separated from the headquarters of the parent firm. Top management is almost certainly separated from operating realities. And all these people think less and less of each subsidiary and more of the conglomerate as a whole. Some of these large firms are very slow to change, and they exhibit many of the same characteristics of large government bureaucracies, avoiding risks and focusing on stability rather than on creativity and initiative. This desire to avoid risks is one reason behind the so-called takeover fever, which has once again gripped the land and is, I think, the cause of the existing economic concentration.

Buying an established firm is less risky than starting a new one, and selling a small business is often less risky than taking your chances in the rough-and-tumble marketplace with corporations that are much larger and have much greater control over the marketplace. But the effects of the takeover trend in the economy are given mixed reviews even by the experts.

Government subsidies, patent policies, contract policies, bail-out legislation, and restrictive regulation operates to continue to encourage increasing concentration. First, the tax code encourages growth for its own sake, but only rewards, in many cases, those big enough to grow even more. One example is the investment tax credit—a federal subsidy to businesses for buying equipment, to the tune of over $8 billion per year. According to the Treasury Department, over 70 percent of the benefits of this tax break go to less than 1 percent of the nation's corporations, those with assets of $100 million or more. Second, the government shies away from enforcing antitrust principles at home and promoting free trade principles abroad. Instead, it often embraces policies of restrictionism, as well as protectionism and subsidization, often at the expense of more efficient and aggressive competitors. Finally, government regulation falls hardest on the small business. The burden of compliance costs makes many smaller agriculture and business groups vulnerable to corporate acquisition. Big firms, because of their market power, can more easily pass the cost of government compliance on to consumers in the form of higher prices. There is growing support for deregulation of America's businesses, at least those which have been traditionally regulated in the past; removing price controls and diminishing the power of the regulatory bureaucracy is what is demanded. This trend, I think, reflects a new appreciation of the costs imposed by inefficient and unnecessary government on the private sector. It indicates a renewed conviction that competition may be the best regulator.

But we must ensure that when price controls are lifted and regulations are phased out, there is, in its place, a truly competitive market. It makes little sense to substitute one set of arbitrary price setters for another. As a lawmaker, I am frustrated continually by the ready acceptance of a regulated market place by too many large companies purportedly committed to free enterprise in exchange for protection from genuine competition and real market principles. In my view, to call for deregulation without some measure of deconcentration assumes the existence of an open and competitive marketplace. Unfortunately, in too many cases this is not true. Antiinflation programs, based on supposedly free markets and relying on fiscal and monetary constraints, have failed. One of the reasons is that many corporations and labor unions have enough power to exact demands in excess of what could be achieved under conditions of active competition. The existence of such powers helps to explain, at least in part, why President Nixon's wage and price controls ended in some regards as failures in 1971. In a competitive market, firms could not raise their prices in a recession without a drop in sales and profits, because they can administer the price with their so-called competitors.

Many corporations do this because they know that government will take action to pump up demand. The government must do so or risk compromising the goal of economic growth with full employment. Admittedly, the relation between concentration and inflation is complex, but I think it can be shown that concentration contributes directly to the cost of living. For example, Dr. Frederick M. Scherer, formerly chief economist for the Federal Trade Commission's bureau of competition, estimates that monopoly profits effect an income redistribution on the order of 3 percent of the GNP from the consuming public to the stockholders of the monopoly corporations.[1] There are certainly competing theories about industrial concentration. The evidence clearly persuades me that the level of concentration that does exist exacerbates the problem of inflation in the midst of recession, which continues to bedevil our economy. If the primary strength of our economy is competition, then I think it is time to come to grips with its primary weakness.

Inefficient industry structures, which stifle competition, invite government regulation to protect the public. The petroleum and natural gas industry provides, I think, a clearer illustration of some of the points I have been trying to make. This industry is in my judgment, and in the judgment of others, heavily concentrated. It is also heavily regulated in terms of its prices, at the present time *and* in recent years. Now I have supported deregulation in this industry, but to the degree that deregulation occurs, I think it should be coupled with deconcentration, to open up a more competitive market place. The structure of this industry is evidence of a point at which legal and economic meanings of monopoly somewhat diverge. No single firm has an unusually large share of the market in production, transportation, refining, and marketing. Yet there is in the minds of many a shared monopoly, a closed system in which sellers are so few that together they often tend to act as one. This is especially true of the petroleum sector of that industry.

While there are thousands of firms in the oil business, only about twenty are vertically integrated, involved in every aspect of the industry, from finding crude oil to selling gasoline. Through an intricate web of intra-corporate ties, a myriad of cooperative arrangements and joint venture, these firms control upwards to 90 percent of the oil flowing from the wellhead to the pump. Many joint ventures go beyond the sharing of the risks of exploration and searching for new reserves. In 1974, an international joint refining and production venture owned by Standard Oil of California and Texaco called CalTex accounted for 60 percent of Standard's profits. Seven major firms own the Trans-Alaska oil pipeline. Aramco, which produces much of the crude oil in Saudi Arabia, is a joint venture of Mobil, Texaco, Standard of California, and Exxon. One study found that fourteen of the largest oil companies had joint ventures with all of the remaining nineteen firms. In each of these cases, the majors sit down together to discuss policies, prices, supplies, planning and investment, and other vital aspects of their business, or at least of that joint venture.

Is that how a free market is supposed to work? It does not need to be a conspiracy for major anticompetitive behavior among the major oil companies to take place. I think that waiting for evidence of a so-called smoking gun is one reason why antitrust legislation has failed to curb growing antitrust concentration, not to mention the amount of time and resources that go into these antitrust actions. In the oil industry and others, market power is concentrated and entry barriers are substantial. Dominant firms naturally recognize their mutual interdependence. They understand that aggressive, independent competitive behavior leads only to lower prices and erodes profits. Major integrated oil firms understand that the vertically integrated system will help preserve their dominance, even if they are less efficient than their nonintegrated rivals. Let me go very briefly into some detail to explain why the major integrated oil firms have, in my judgment, excessive market power. I am using this industry as an example of the principles I am talking about. Vertical integration of petroleum is an obstacle to active competition, particularly in the refining area.

The competitive advantage of the integrated refiner can be overcome only if a newcomer can enter the industry on a vertically integrated basis, which of course is almost impossible. In other words, a newcomer must first acquire some control over crude oil reserves and then a pipeline before being able to compete with an integrated refiner on an equal basis. By raising the cost of entry this way, vertical integration is a barrier to competition that few can afford to hurdle. The result is that integrated firms are able to charge prices that do not necessarily reflect their minimum costs. There are no more huge reserves of crude oil to be found in this country. Therefore, newcomers, as well as the established nonintegrated firms, are critically dependent on the majors for their supply of oil, because the vertically integrated major firms provide crude oil to nonintegrated firms and then compete with them in the sale of the refined product.

Even so, owners and operators of independent refineries know that they can spot some of the major refiners a dollar a barrel and still beat them in the competitive marketplace in terms of the efficiency of their refineries. The integrated firm can simply stay ahead of the competition in refining by just raising the price of the raw material, the crude oil. I ask if this is the way that the free market is supposed to work?

The major integrated firms dominate the industry not because they are efficient, although some of them are, but because, as a result of the structure of the industry, they exercise control far beyond what they themselves produce. Further, because the integrated firm has a much larger cash flow, it need not focus on profit maximization in petroleum alone. Mobil's multibillion dollar acquisition of Montgomery Ward is often cited as evidence of this. The integrated firm can afford to keep capital and raw materials off the open market and inside the closed system that it shares with other firms.

Integrated firms also control the bulk of natural gas flow and distribution through joint ownership of both wells and pipelines. Although thousands of nonintegrated firms drill over 90 percent of the natural gas in this country, they drill most often on property owned by the majors. Major integrated firms are therefore able to control the rate, production, and sale of the product. The eight largest firms alone control about 75 percent of the natural gas reaching the consumer, directly or indirectly, about three times that collectively controlled by the thousands of other firms in the business. I think it is easy to understand why a number of people and organizations in this country, not the least of whom is the current President of the United States, believe that the major oil and gas producers have excessive power. These firms have the means and the material incentive to withhold large amounts of new gas in order to prevent a deregulated price from falling. But the President's suggested remedy, continued governmental price control, ignores, I think, the fundamental truth of that industry, which is that the operation of the industry is controlled by its structure.

Continuing government regulation treats the symptom, but not the disease. The result of deregulation of the price of natural gas and petroleum without deconcentration takes the power to control prices and set production away from the government and puts it into the hands of the major oil and gas producers. The essence of economic power is the ability to exploit mutual interdependence among supposed rivals and to insulate oneselves from the rigors of competitive markets. Major oil companies, by this definition, have enormous economic power, and they are extending their power into other non-energy-related fields, primarily through mergers and acquisition. The government, as I have suggested, has contributed to this through leasing policies, import quotas, tax incentives, and a myriad of other public policies directed toward a highly concentrated industry.

So I join in criticizing government intervention and calling for deregulation. The result of 40 years of government regulation is that a handful of oil giants, who are, of course, multinationals, run the industry as a de facto government sustained cartel. What should be done? To simply deconcentrate without deregulation would make equally little sense. But I do not believe that it is an either/or choice. If the ultimate objective in this country is a free market, in the end, a decentralized power structure is needed that can preserve that market. Of course, we should attack on both fronts: deregulation combined with deconcentration.

I think one other point should be emphasized. Even if the government is labeled the principal culprit, is that not largely a reflection of the power of distribution in our economy.

After all, economics and politics do not operate in separate universes. Economic power, almost without exception, translates into political power. Is it not imperative to strive for a decentralization of that power structure, precisely to reduce the likelihood that government will become the handmaiden of private interests. The problem of economic concentration does not concern only economic issues. There are social and political implications as well. It is difficult to measure the effect of innovation, or risk taking, or large-scale organization, productivity, critical thinking, or community life. Even if economics argued for one giant American oil company, I doubt that most Americans would support such a policy. The threat of the integrity to the political process would be too great. The potential for abuse in the marketplace would be too great. The petroleum industry is an example of an inefficient industry structure resulting both from government regulatory policies and the so-called rules of the game. Be it the dictates of the competitive market, pressures from imports or substitutes, or the discipline of yardstick competition, it is these forces that policymakers must try to reinforce where they exist or build into the economy where they are deficient or do not exist at all. The policy throughout should be to produce market structures that will compel performance in the public interest.

No one can pretend to have all the answers and certainly I do not, but I have introduced a bill called the Competition Review Act, which I think is one way to attack an extremely complex and important issue. This act would focus on developing sensible answers to some of the problems we are here to discuss. The bill would establish, first of all, a competition review commission to study the impact of the government's laws and regulatory policies on competition in our economy. It would focus on concentration in both management and labor. It would develop recommendations for legislative changes and regulatory modifications necessary to strengthen a competitive economy. The commission study would be, quite simply, the most comprehensive study ever undertaken of the American economy. The result would be a resolution of some of the competing theories of economic concentration and ultimate assurance that whatever policy the government pursues, it does so in a consistent manner rather than having, as we do today, various government programs operating more often than not at cross purposes. But in the interim, I think we should apply free market principles wherever we can, wherever they will work, such as in industries like petroleum and steel. In the interim, we can begin to substitute regulation for competition in prices and in those certain industries and in other industries, such as airlines, transportation, and communications. It is not enough to sit back and wait for the market to straighten itself out. The steel industry is evidence of that. So is the oil business, and so is the rising cost of living.

The competitive private sector is not just the result of negative or antigrowth policies; it should be the result of a totally integrated approach on all levels of public policy. Such an approach would necessarily make deregulation a necessary component. It would also include deconcentration as a necessary component. It is both feasible and desirable to pursue such an approach. Our long-term economic goals should be to guarantee long-term economic opportunities for all.

The first step toward that goal is to ensure a healthy environment for small and medium-sized businesses. I think it is time we choose either to preserve inefficient power structures or take the fundamentally conservative step of decentralizing decision making in order to put more power in the hands of individuals and less in their economic and political institutions. To do otherwise would be to betray the economic principles on which this nation was originally founded. Rather than betray, I think we should be true to the principle espoused by Thomas Jefferson, who said that the "way to have good and safe government. . .is to divide it among the many."[2] We also should consider the words of Franklin Delano Roosevelt: [T]he system of free enterprise for profit has not failed in this generation, but [rather] it has not yet been tried."[3]

Harold Demsetz's Presentation

Senator Hart offers us a deal; not a great deal, but a deal nonetheless. We can have deregulation if we take deconcentration. The proposition offered to us by Senator Hart is in fact a poor and dangerous bargain, well deserving of a resounding ''no deal'' for four reasons.

First, great improvements from deregulation are possible whether or not other industries are deconcentrated. I will not address the question of what the proper structures of regulated industries should be; since they have been regulated by the government for so long, I have no way of knowing their proper structures. But it is certainly not the case that we must deconcentrate the automobile industry, the steel industry, the computer industry, or any other industry in order to derive benefits from deregulating the oil industry and a host of other industries that could be mentioned.

Second, Congress is an incompetent but dangerous institution for determining the structure of American industry. The superior institution for guiding industrial structure already is in place if only we will use it; I will refer to it later.

Third, enforced deconcentration will raise costs and prices and decrease efficiency. Further, it will not reduce inflation.

Fourth, deconcentration cannot be accomplished without a dangerous *increase* in regulation. Therefore, if there is a public policy to deconcentrate industries, Senator Hart will be unable to deliver deregulation.

Presumably, the attractiveness of a deconcentration policy to Senator Hart is his belief that deconcentrated industries are more competitive or more efficient than concentrated industries. This view is unsupportable in theory or fact. Consider the following real problems in judging the degree of competition and its relationship to industry structure. Suppose a firm were contemplating the innovation of a new soft drink. It must take a significant risk in research, development, product resources, and marketing. Even if the product it brings to the market is a significant improvement over existing beverages, it can receive a return on its investment only if imitators are prevented from completely duplicating in content and name (and even in bottle shape) the product developed by this firm. Without patent, trademark, and copyright protection, such investments in invention, innovation, and the creation of consumer good will would diminish; if anyone can imitate and produce this soft drink or other invention after an innovator develops it, there can be little profit in investing in innovation.

We therefore provide legal protection to a firm's right to its product. But by so doing, we also create the opportunity for a successful product developer to win a large share of the market, making the industry more concentrated in structure and able to earn high profits while doing so. To say that effective competition requires the breaking up of such a firm is to penalize competitive investment in risky innovation and thereby reduce such investment. To what degree should the incentive to competitively innovate be reduced in order to reduce the market share of successful innovating firms? The probability that Congress can provide a good answer is considerably smaller than the probability that it can invent a good soft drink (meanwhile the Russians find it desirable to import Pepsi-Cola).

The problem goes beyond product innovation and into product technique. The automobile industry became concentrated when Henry Ford risked assembly line production of an automobile produced for the mass of American consumers at a price substantially below the handcrafted automobiles that were then being produced. His success basically altered the making of automobiles, away from handcrafting, to a process that brings the automobile within the budget of most American families. In the process, by dramatically lowering the price of automobiles, Ford acquired a large market share and high profits. Should such success be penalized by imposing an arbitrary limit on market share? Should the incentive to introduce radically different methods of production be reduced in order to limit the market's share of successful firms? The probability that Congress can provide an answer is considerably lower than the probability that it can produce automobiles at a low cost (meanwhile the Russians seek the aid of the American automobile industry when setting up automobile plants in the USSR).

The problem goes beyond product innovation and new product technique; it extends to managerial organization. Part of the reason for the success of DuPont, General Motors, General Electric, and other firms has been the creation of new techniques of centralized budgeting with decentralized management of corporate divisions. These methods provide flexibility while maintaining accountability to the central profit center. This allows the lower costs associated with large volume production to be achieved, while preventing bureaucratic red tape from dissipating the savings. The payoff in reducing bureaucratic red tape is achieved primarily from the large volume of operations. To what degree should the incentive to cut red tape be reduced by preventing growth of those firms which seek to increase their share of the market by cutting red tape? The probability that Congress can provide a good answer to this question, we all know, is zero (and the Russians have not yet asked the U.S. Congress for advice on cutting red tape).

Schumpeter had the right idea when he contrasted the kind of competition Senator Hart seeks (typified by competing farmers, who, by the way, are primary benefactors from government protection) and the kind of industrial competition that Senator Hart attacks. Schumpeter said, "But in Capitalist reality, as distinguished from its textbook picture, it is not that kind of competition that counts [the kind Senator Hart wants to promote], but the competition from the new commodity, the new technology, the new source of supply, the new type of organization, the largest scale unit of control, for instance. Competition which commands a decisive cost advantage, which strikes not at the margins of outputs of existing firms, but at their foundations and their very lives. That kind of competition is as much more effective than the other as a bombardment is in forcing a door.''[4]

From the foregoing, I would like to draw conclusions. First, when the many dimensions that competition can take are recognized (invention, quality, production and change, price, and so forth), the relationship between competition and industry structure is hardly clear. Second, Congress simply does not know, and is not likely ever to know, the proper structure of American industries. Government vacillation about the proper structure of industries is fully revealed by contrasting the positions toward industrial concentration taken by England and the United States during the 1930s and those urged upon us today. The 1930s vogue in England was to rationalize industry, to limit the number of firms in the industries. In coal mining, the English government compelled consolidation and cartelization, and from 1932 until after World War II, it was wholeheartedly committed to achieving the same results for cotton and steel and a host of other industries. In the United States, until the Supreme Court intervened, the Roosevelt administration attempted to use the NRA to achieve the same results. Now we are told today that Congress should seek to deconcentrate industry.

Well, a plague on both your houses. Both directions of interferences with industry structure are unwarranted, being based mainly on ignorance directed by the political pressures of the times. Ignorance and political culpability are good reasons for denying to government the power to restructure industries.

A wiser policy is to increase our reliance on the test of survival in the marketplace. We might ask, How does industrial concentration fare in the market place? There have been several careful studies of the degree to which an industry's output is concentrated in the hands of a few large firms. Those estimates reveal that in 1900, one-third of value added in manufacturing came from the industries in which the four largest firms accounted for 50 percent or more of output. By 1963, the corresponding figure was still one-third. Between 1947 and 1970, average concentration for an unchanging group of manufacturing industries rose from 41 to 43 percent when measured by relative shipments produced by the four largest companies. It is true that industrial concentration across several markets appears to have been increasing over time. The largest firms in manufacturing, across a wide variety of industry, acquired a greater percentage of the assets of the manufacturing sector, as was correctly pointed out by Senator Hart. But what he did not talk about when he talked about those 200 largest firms acquiring a larger share of manufacturing assets is that it was the second, not the first hundred largest. He also failed to point out that the manufacturing sector hardly makes up the whole of the business sector. And he did not note that most of the increase in overall concentration stems from the fact that American firms have expanded abroad. The size of firms measured without adjustment for overseas operations gives a false picture of increasing concentration on the domestic scene. In the United States market, the 200 largest firms have not increased their share of manufacturing assets by nearly the amount suggested by official statistics.

Several studies have been produced in recent years that give good reason for confidence in the ability of market competition to select for survival those industry structures which yield output at lowest cost to consumers. These independent studies, published recently in professional journals, are based on data secured by the government of the United States and Australia. They offer strong statistical evidence that in highly concentrated industries, the largest firms produce at the lowest cost. But in unconcentrated industries, large firms possess no cost advantages. This suggests that industry structures, unprotected by government regulation, reflect the underlying cost of producers, and that an industry becomes concentrated in structure when some firm (Ford Motors, in my previous example) becomes large as a result of its success in achieving cost or product breakthroughs, and not otherwise. Evidence published recently by Sam Peltzman shows that increases in industry concentration have been correlated significantly with reduction in both the unit cost and the price of the products produced. [5]

With such underlying cost and product considerations at work determining industry structure, it is a delusion to believe that a program of deconcentration can be a one time only affair. Cost considerations and innovations will compel reconstitution of many concentrated structures. To make a deconcentration policy effective, Congress will need to regulate the containment of successful firms. A public policy of deconcentration therefore implies government planning to control the growth of business firms. The most likely consequence of such a policy will be to penalize success and efficiency. Prices of products will be increased, both because of the lack of incentives to invest and because of the lack of incentives to reduce cost, the advantages of which cannot be secured because firms will not be allowed to grow without facing dissolution. Such detailed control of economic activity dims the prospective of the continued functioning of a free economy.

The proffered exchange of deconcentration for deregulation will become a sham, because regulation will increase and not decrease. There are ample opportunities for Congress to help ensure the competitiveness of the American economy without the very serious dangers that I draw your attention to. It can begin by stopping its efforts to keep cost-effective imports out of the country. The government could, by this single stroke, eliminate any need for concern about industrial concentration; the world is full of producers ready and able to compete in this market. The government can continue by stopping payment to farmers to reduce output (hardly a concentrated industry, I might point out). And if it is truly concerned about competition, the government can remove labor union exemptions from the antitrust laws. Finally, without the least concern about industrial concentration, the government can end its efforts to cartelize industry through the regulatory commissions. With all these unexercised options before Congress, Senator Hart will forgive my skepticism about his attempt to deconcentrate industry.

But even a well-educated Congress cannot know the implications of alternative industry structures. Because of this economic ignorance, economic considerations necessarily give way to political tests of the desirability of particular growth patterns of firms. (The oil industry gets attacked because it is politically popular for it to be attacked; there has not been a single study that demonstrates that the industry will be more efficient if it is broken apart.) A public policy toward industry structure will thus move us measurably down the road to fascism.

Gary Hart's Rebuttal

Tempted as I am to rise to the bait of defending Congress, I will not take the tactic of clouding the issue and diverting people's attention, as Professor Demsetz does by pursuing the popular political course of criticizing Congress instead of the oil industry. With regard to what Professor Demsetz calls "stolen power," I would point out in my own defense that I have been in office only 3 years and can be responsible only for some, not all, of that stolen power. Professor Demsetz also suggests that the offer I made should be rejected because he doubts that I could deliver deregulation. Now a senator from a slightly populated state rarely delivers anything—but the realities of political power being what they are, all the senators in the country probably could not deliver deregulation even if they were inclined to do so. I understand Professor Demsetz as saying that because we cannot deregulate such industries as automobiles and electronics, we should not pursue the deregulation and deconcentration of other industries such as oil. It is not entirely clear why that follows, but nonetheless, it is a point that deserves pursuit at some later time.

Professor Demsetz quoted that the true competition was not so much price, but rather the competition from the new products, new technology, and so forth. In that regard, I would refer once again to the steel industry, pointing out first of all that very little innovation comes out of concentrated industries. For example, from a study showing sixty of our most important inventions over recent years, only half came from independent inventors, and substantially less than half came from corporate research. Much more money is placed in marketing and advertising than in research and development; in fact, two-thirds of our research money comes from the federal government. The steel industry, as Professor Demsetz and I would both agree, is an example of the devastating conditions that can occur under a regulated industry; as a result of concentration, the steel industry spends only 0.7 percent on research. In technology, the giants of that industry lag far behind their domestic rivals, as well as their smaller foreign competitors. For example, the one major technological breakthrough in the steel industry in recent years, the oxygen furnace, was invented in 1950 by a very small foreign firm less than one-third the size of a single plant of U.S. Steel. In addition, despite the fact that this invention involved a cost savings of $5 per ton, it took the giants almost 15 years to adopt it. Finally, that same evil Congress that Professor Demsetz talks about is constantly seeing corporations batter down its doors asking for tax breaks, subsidies, government bail-out, or protection from foreign competition. Congress is mostly responsible for the unholy mess our tax system is in. Those who would like to preserve and protect our business structure as it now is—which has been described as state capitalism or private socialism—should look very carefully at the role that the contemptible Congress has played, a role that in my view goes too far to preserve a degree of concentration that is unhealthy.

My thinking about this type of concentrated power is from Thomas Jefferson. I know I risk being outdated and anachronistic, but it is a fundamental philosophic conviction of mine that concentrated power is not what this country was founded on. I realize the fundamental changes in economic life that have taken place in this country; I am realistic enough to know that an automobile manufacturer has to have 10 percent of the market to compete and that at this point no one has the money to get into that game. I am not saying that big is bad and small is beautiful. Some people think the unions have too much power too. My point is that the type of power the unions have too much of, the companies also have too much of.

Every corporation in this country is chartered by the government in the sense that their power is given to them by acts of the government. And I agree that if they ask for political power, it should be refused. But the point is that in 90 percent of the issues where unions and businesses have an interest, they are on the same side of the table. Labor and management only knock heads over the contract; once they go to Washington, it is hand in hand. Look at the Clean Air Act. Labor and management were in Washington standing cheek by jowl. That is power.

I have focused on the petroleum industry, as opposed to other, more concentrated industries because it is the characteristic of vertical integration that I am concerned with. From the ground to the gas pump, about eighteen companies control 90 percent of our petroleum, 75 percent of the pipelines, and 80 percent of the refinery capacity. It is not just one company, it is the aggregate of control; these companies have all sorts of arrangements among themselves. The critical point at which we must sever the control of these companies in order to increase competition is exploration. We would still have joint ventures, and if divested, the prices would be quite large.

Harold Demsetz's Rebuttal

A deconcentration bill that will transfer a tremendous amount of power to the place that has the most power already, Washington, D.C., is a bad idea. I am not a defender of big business; I do not think that the steel industry should be protected by this trigger-price regulation by the government. Government regulation is one of the things that has led to an increase in demand for domestic steel. I lay the fault for this at the doorsteps of Congress and the steel industry.

Everyone has a right to petition Congress for a redress of their grievances, but sometimes Congress should not listen. The instances where government has interceded most have not been for big business. While there have been pro-industrial tariffs, it has been with agriculture, the unions, and the licensed professions, where a large number of votes are at stake, that the government more frequently interceded and offered protection. And if anyone thinks that decentralizing the oil industry will reduce the number of appeals made by that industry for protection, they are only kidding themselves. It is not the automobile industry but the United Auto Workers who are petitioning Congress for protection from Japanese cars. If we are worried about the inefficiency of the steel industry, we should not keep foreign steel out. This is the real test of whether the steel industry is efficient or not. And if we are worried about oil companies, look at the Texas Railroad Commission (TRC), where the petroleum industry is greatly regulated. The TRC works mainly to the benefit of the small oil producers, not the large ones. Look at the way the federal government hands out entitlements to import oil; they are handed out disproportionately to the small producers. The atomistically designed industry has the greatest political power, not the large firm. The large, concentrated firms are so politically unpopular that they can work only behind the scenes; they can never work out in the open the way the unconcentrated industries do.

It is incorrect to say that big business readily passes cost increases on. There have been many statistical studies showing the relation between the concentration of the industry and the rate of change of product prices. The overwhelming preponderance of the evidence in those studies is that there is no relationship. In fact, the findings of some of the studies show that prices increase more during an inflation in unconcentrated than in concentrated industries. With regard to the point about not being able to attack a monopoly's profit margin, that has nothing to do with inflation. If there is a monopoly, it is tacking the monopoly margin on every year. What we are interested in is where the price goes up the fastest. It does not go up the fastest in the concentrated industries.

With regard to the tremendous intertwining of monopoly power that exists in Senator Hart's mind about the oil industry, my final comment is that the oil industry never recorded profits that were not commensurate with those of the average manufacturing industry. It is not clear to me where the oil industry is using this monopoly power, because it is certainly not in profits.

That all businessmen want to be the top producer in their industry is not inconsistent with competition. We are all competing to be number one or two. Competing well is how a businessman becomes number one—by producing better products at lower costs, not by buying other firms. Some firms went bankrupt trying to merge their way to the top—merger can make you number last.

Vertical integration does not expedite monopoly. Monopoly depends on how exclusively one can control any one point of distribution. Most of the oil pipelines Senator Hart speaks of are common carriers. Even if we tore the oil companies apart, the price of oil would still be set by OPEC.

Notes

1. Frederick Sherer, *Industrial Market Structure and Economic Performance* (Chicago: Rand McNally & Co., 1970), p. 409.

2. *The Writings of Thomas Jefferson* (Washington, D.C.: The Thomas Jefferson Memorial Association, 1905), p. xxiii.

3. *The Public Papers and Addresses of Franklin D. Roosevelt* (1938 vol.), (New York: Macmillan Co., 1941), p. 320.

4. Joseph A. Schumpeter, *Capitalism, Socialism, and Democracy,* 6 (New York, N.Y.: Harper & Bros., 1950), p. 84.

5. Sam Peltzman, "The Gains and Losses from Industrial Concentration," *Journal of Law and Economics,* 22 (1977): 191.

6

Should the Legal Services Corporation Be Abolished?

Howard Phillips and
Earl Johnson, Jr.

Howard Phillips's Presentation

In order to discuss the Legal Services Program, I think it is well to spend a moment or two reviewing its structure and its history. The Legal Services Program was founded in the middle 1960s by people from the then Office of Economic Opportunity. It was established on a grant basis, later receiving a statutory basis under the Economic Opportunity Act. Its funding grew from a level of under $1 million a year in the first year of its existence to $71 million a year when Richard Nixon left office. When Gerald Ford left office, its funding was $125 million per year. Now we are speaking of a legal services funding in excess of $300 million per year.

Because when you have a free supply of legal services, you can always expect the demand for such free services to increase, I am sure that we will hear for years to come a cry in Congress that we need more money for legal services, since there are as yet unmet demands.

The Legal Services Program today functions under the aegis of a national corporation, the directors of which are chosen by the President of the United States, subject to his appointments being confirmed in the Senate. But that corporation is primarily an administrative body, and the program really works on the local level through some 315 private nonprofit corporations, governed by policy boards which, for the most part at least, are self-designated and self-perpetuating.

One of my principal concerns with the Legal Services Program is that in many parts of the country, seats on these policy boards (which govern the operations of the programs locally) are assigned to groups of a political character (not a partisan character, although inevitably there will be people with partisan views on some of the boards). Rather, seats are assigned in area after area to spokesmen for groups such as the National Organization for Women, the National Lawyers Guild, the United Auto Workers, the National Welfare Rights Organization, and so forth.

I would argue that this is a form of public financing of political activity of all kinds, but I am particularly opposed to arbitrarily assigned public financing that is supportive of merely one side of the argument.

On the outset, it is important to bear in mind what the Legal Services Program is, and what it is not. The Legal Services Program, in my view, is not a poor people's program; it is a lawyer's program. It is not a program to impartially serve justice, but one that uses public funds to seek political change outside of the political process (not just through the courts, but through grass-roots lobbying organizations, paid legislative agents, voter registration efforts, public agents, and lobbying personnel of state and federal agencies and legislative bodies).

In its operation, employees of local projects, funded by the federal Legal Services Program, have been taxpayer-funded advocates and organizers of such political causes as quotas, welfare rights, unions of unemployed workers, student protests and dissence, Indian land claims, proposals for graduated state income taxes, the Equal Rights Amendment, prisoners rights movements, rent strikes, and so forth.

In fact, I would argue that there has not been a significant policy area during the past 10 or 15 years in which Legal Service attorneys have not played a significant role. By their own acknowledgment, Legal Service attorneys were involved in some fifty-three forced busing cases in different parts of the United States. Legal Services attorneys around the country were involved in a series of cases that presaged the Supreme Court abortion decision. Certainly in the area of food stamps, the Food Research Action Center (which is one of the Legal Services' so-called back-up centers) played a key role in significantly expanding the Food Stamp Program from its relatively limited start in the middle 1960s, where 1 in 400 families was served, to a point today, where it has an annual budget of nearly $6 billion.

Under both the corporation and the Office for Economic Opportunity (OEO), employees of taxpayer-funded Legal Services Projects have been in the forefront of action for radical political change. They have advanced the priorities of those who control the program, all the while self-righteously proclaiming to speak for the poor.

What is wrong with the Legal Services Program, and how can that wrong be cured? Well, I used to be of the view that the way to reform the Legal Services Program was by placing restrictions on the permitted activities of legal services attorneys. I have, however, noticed that when there was a restriction on lobbying, that restriction was sometimes circumvented by lobbying in what was called "outside hours" or during "outside practice of law." I have also noticed that despite eligibility requirements, it has been quite easy for these requirements to be waived, altered, or circumvented.

I also have observed that, even though the program does represent many individual clients, there is a significant focus on what is called "law reform" and, within that area, emphasis on such things as lobbying, drafting model legislation, test case litigation, and the like.

In my view, one of the most insidious areas of activity involving the federal Legal Services Program is the area of organizing and representing groups of a fundamentally political character, involved in women's liberation, or Vietnam war protest, or student dissence, or whatever it may be. I do not think that it is healthy for the federal government to subsidize attorneys from one point of view who are politically active. This seems to be a violation of the civil liberties of the taxpayer who believes that he should be able to control the policies that govern his life through his personal choices and the ballot box. Of course, it is true that increasingly we have become a society where policy is set for better or for worse in the courts and the judicial area, but I think that it is most unfair to give extra advantage to merely one point of view in the courts, as is the case with the Legal Services Program.

One of the unstated premises of the Legal Services Program is that people without economic resources should be uniformly considered in class terms as having an easily defined, economically determinable stake in the outcome of public-policy questions. I have met Legal Services attorneys (one after another) who say that poor people are defined only in economic terms and that the only economic solution for poor people is one or another kind of redistribution of resources, whether it is a guaranteed annual income, the ability to withhold rent payments, or whatever else.

One of the problems with the Legal Services Program is the staff attorney system itself. In the private practice of law, attorneys are retained by individuals, and because the individuals pay their fees, such lawyers are accountable economically as well as psychologically to the problems, priorities, and concerns of the individuals they represent. But by vesting the power of purchase in the provider of legal services rather than in the consumer (which the federal Legal Services Program does), the situation is turned upside down. All bureaucracies are inherently self-serving, whether they are medical bureaucracies, education bureaucracies, or conservative bureaucracies. However altruistic they may be, they all inevitably wind up advancing their personal notions of the public good.

He who pays the piper calls the tune. Staff attorneys will play the tune for those who pay their guaranteed annual salaries, namely, the board and staff leadership of the Legal Services Project by which they are employed, not the clients among whom they may pick and choose without losing a dime of income. If any service is free, the demand will be greater than the supply. This enhances the position of the provider, who is then required to determine which demand shall be satisfied.

Furthermore, with salary assured, the provider may well determine that it is more efficient to serve broad social and law reform objectives than to waste time on the mundane concerns of individuals whose problems lack a broad political connotation.

Now hear what I am saying; I am not suggesting that Legal Services attorneys are neglecting the problems of individual clients. I recognize that many individual clients are served by officials of the Legal Services

Program. What I am saying is that a substantial number of Legal Services employees do consider it inefficient to devote a substantial portion of their time to individual representation when they can solve problems broadly through class action suits, test case litigation, and other types of law reform.

You do not have to believe me as the source of this. In *Public Interest Magazine* a couple of years ago, there was an article by a man named Brill, who worked for the San Francisco Neighborhood Legal Assistance Foundation and described a situation in which the local units of the foundation were interested in serving particular clients and the central unit focused primarily on what it perceived to be broad law reform activities. To this end, many in the central unit would conclude, "Why not reject that divorce case, in favor of an extra week of research on a fine point of law? Why not reduce the client caseload in order to take a case on appeal? Why not divert resources in the direction of group representation and law reform, but not into legislation, lobbying, and state legislatures whenever an eligible client is found?" Even if the client has to be created (which is the case many times), this does happen.

I have pulled, from various publications and books, quotations from Legal Services attorneys talking about how clients were created, whether they were American Indian Movement chapters in South Dakota or prisoners' rights organizations or whatever. Indeed, I recall reading in the *Clearinghouse Review* the boast that throughout the United States, in excess of 500 chapters of the National Welfare Rights Organization were constituted with the help of federally funded Legal Services projects. And I recall reading an evaluation model when I came to OEO that spelled out the basis on which local Legal Services projects were to be awarded levels of funding in the future, one criteria of which was how well they had served local welfare rights objectives.

In effect, what we have is a nationwide law office with a nationwide network of Legal Service programs. Legal Services personnel can pick and choose among circuits to decide where litigation will be initiated, targeting those circuits where the incumbent judge may be inclined to have an ideologically favorable attitude. Once again, I do not wish to demean the judicial profession; I do not mean to suggest that all judges are motivated by philosophical bias rather than by the law. But I believe that any citizen who has observed what has been happening in the courts can only conclude that members of the judiciary are human beings who put their pants on one leg at a time like everyone else. However much they attempt to limit their decisions to their reading of the law, that reading is inevitably colored by their views on the nature of man, their philosophical outlook, and their moral and political beliefs.

If you are part of a nationwide network of attorneys you can say that you have a better chance of getting a favorable decision in one judicial circuit as opposed to another. And if you are in a position to pick and choose among clients, you are in a position to do something about it.

What of the party who lacks a free lawyer, for example, the small business man? Harassed by a plaintiff who is backed by a financially unlimited supply of representation, the defendant businessman will quickly discover that even if he wins in court, he may very well be destroyed financially by the burden of privately paid legal fees.

Over the course of a few years working for the federal government, I personally had the opportunity to talk with dozens upon dozens of farmers, landlords, and small businessmen who (whether or not their causes were just or unjust) were put in a position of being sued by Legal Services attorneys who had no economic constraint on their performance. In these cases, the small businessman did not have his attorney's fees paid by the government, and very often had no alternative but to yield to the litigative demands made on him or face the alternative of financial ruin.

I would argue that is an extremely unfair system and that the answer lies not in providing more staff attorneys for the people being sued, because the old story of the lawyer in the small town who had no business until another lawyer moved into the same town and then both of them did very well is so true. I am afraid that this is the kind of situation that would result if we simply tried to remedy one problem with an additional dose of the same elixir that caused the problem in the first place.

The Legal Services Program operates through local projects that assign seats to essentially political organizations. If you, as a liberal, were confronted with a situation in which the federal government were assigning dollars to private Legal Services Programs whose boards were composed of people assigned through the bylaws to the Conservative Caucus, the Libertarian Party, the National Right to Work Committee, the Heritage Foundation, Phyllis Schlafly's Eagle Forum, or whatever it might be, you would be understandably upset; it would be wrong, in my view, to use federal funds in that way.

I hope that if Conservatives are ever in a position of power, they will resist the temptation to fund their political causes at the expense of others; but today, we are confronted with the situation in which political liberals control a substantial amount of Legal Services funding in various parts of the country.

In 1813, Thomas Jefferson and John Adams were engaged in a lively correspondence, and in the course of that correspondence, Jefferson wrote, "The artificial aristocracy is a mischievous ingredient in government, and provision should be made to prevent its ascendency."[1] In other words, man should be allowed to govern himself, and he should not be ruled by a small elite.

I believe the real problem with the Legal Services Program is that the people who occupy positions of leadership in that program, nationally and locally, believe that they know what is best for the country. Unfortunately, from the standpoint of those who disagree with their policy conclusions, they have been given millions of dollars to advance (in many cases, unrebutted) their notion of the public good, not just in the courts, but in administrative corridors, administrative agencies, newspapers, ballot referendums, and so forth, and I think that this is extremely unfair. Professor Geoffrey Hazard of Yale Law School made an observation about the Legal Services Program that is worth repeating:

> The question in testcase litigation, as in legislative law reform, boils down to the propriety of constituting a publicly funded agency to lobby for the special benefit of a limited sector of the general community. . . .

> There is a serious if simple question of principle involved, namely, whether government predicated on equal participation of all members of the electorate is compatible with providing some of them with a special political equipage at public expense. . . . [I]n a constitutional regime, partisan political activity is supposed to be a matter of private initiative. [2]

A government that creates agencies to formulate what shall be taken as the people's will is no longer a government by the people. In my view, perhaps the greatest problem facing the United States today, in terms of its political institutions, is what I would call the crisis of accountability. More and more Americans have reached the conclusion that no matter what they do, they are unable to control the uses to which their tax dollars are assigned; they are unable to control the force of public policy through the electoral process. It is quite correct that Congress has abdicated its responsibility and acquiesced in the authority that has been granted to the Legal Services Program. But I would argue that Congress is to be faulted for having delegated policy-setting functions to private organizations that should either be reserved for the marketplace or to the ballot box. Those policy questions threaten to change, in the manner in which they are being pursued, the very nature of the society in which we live.

There was a very interesting article in the current edition of *Regulation Magazine* that talked about our being too litigative in our society and the problem of eroding the autonomous private institutions that give the individual immunity and protection from the authority and monopoly control of the central state. Institutions like schools, the family, and churches are increasingly coming under uniform federal regulation, much of which is being enacted and promulgated by the courts.

I think it is wrong, for example, for Legal Service attorneys to represent children under the age of 18 without parental consent, because that erodes family authority. Also, I think it is wrong for the Legal Services Program to be able to declare that students are eligible clients simply because they are voluntarily unemployed. I think it is wrong for the Legal Services Program to represent prison inmates who are poor because, as a result of a voluntary criminal act, they are in prison. I do not think this is an appropriate use of legal services for the poor.

But the preferred answer, once again, is not regulation. The problem is an economic one, and the solution is an economic one. As long as Legal Services attorneys have guaranteed annual salaries, then the Legal Services Program will be a lawyer's program and not a clients one.

The answer to the Legal Services Program in the short term is to produce a situation in which either through the voluntary activities of the private bar or, if you will, through a voucher system, the power of purchase comes to repose in the consumer of legal services rather than in the provider.

If you move to that different economic system, away from monopoly and central collective decision making of the staff system to the diversity of pluralism, the decentralization of the marketplace, then I am prepared to trust the checks and balances of that marketplace in preference to the types of regulations that are necessary to hold in check the abuses of the present program.

Earl Johnson's Presentation

Mr. Phillips has leveled a shotgun, and it would be difficult to try to deal adequately with each and every pellet he has fired. I have written a book entitled *Justice and Reform* that addresses most of the assaults he launches against the Legal Services Corporation far more adequately than I could do in a half hour.[3]

But I do think that in this limited time we can attempt to consider the philosophic basis of the Legal Services Corporation and the Legal Services Program that it took over in 1974. It is not predicated on some kind of Marxist, radical, or even liberal ideology, rather it is a concept that goes back to our founding fathers and before that to some of the English theoreticians such as John Locke whose ideas shaped the political charter of our country. It goes back to the idea of political equality, not economic equality—the idea that no citizen would give up his sovereignty to the state unless he felt that he was going to have an equal opportunity to participate in the making of the laws under which he was going to live and an equal opportunity to enforce those laws on his own behalf. This is the basis of the program.

But we do have a problem, because political equality is much more complex today than it was at the time of our founding fathers, when almost everybody knew their own congressman, state legislator, the local judges, and so forth and did not have great need of a lawyer. We now live in an era in which lawyers are essential to political equality in this country. It is through lawyers acting as courtroom advocates that we have access to the courts. It is through lawyers acting as legislative advocates that we have access to the legislative process.

Moreover, it also is true that political equality will very often lead to greater economic equality. Put another way, a lack of political equality will often produce much greater economic inequality. If you do not have an advocate to represent you when you are sued by someone, you inevitably lose in court and thus suffer a direct economic loss. For a poor person, this means greater economic inequality. Similarly, if you are unable to advocate in the legislative halls or administrative agencies on the same footing as other people do, you are going to suffer greater economic inequality. Conversely, if you are provided greater political inequality, often greater economic equality, or at least less economic inequality, is produced.

Another source of confusion about the role of the Legal Services Corporation and a cause of some controversy is the way a lawyer promotes our rights to political equality. When you are exercising your rights to full political equality and hire a lawyer, your lawyer does not get up in court and advocate political equality for you. Rather he says, "My client wants money, or property, or whatever." When an attorney advocates in legislative chambers, he does not say, "My client wants political equality," he says, "My client wants a law passed that is going to benefit him." If you are in the lowest income scale, this in fact means that you are going to be arguing for more economic equality. Whether or not the lawyer even believes in greater economic equality, it is his duty to advocate your cause. When implementing his client's right (the conservative right to political equality), it often sounds as if the lawyer is advocating a liberal (or even radical) cause because he is in fact arguing the best interests of his client, which often will happen to be for more welfare, better public housing, and so forth.

Despite Mr. Phillips's attempt to introduce a score of charges, I think that in reality there are only two issues in this particular debate. First, are legal services for the poor a good thing? And second, is the Legal Services Corporation a good way of administering that good thing?

As to the first question, I think we need a little context because Mr. Phillips has attempted to portray this Legal Services Corporation as a huge demon with a budget of $205 million. That is, in fact, a very modest sum. I do not think even Mr. Phillips would quarrel with the idea that low-income people have a need for lawyers. Yet surveys show that under present appropriation, Legal Services lawyers are only able to meet approximately one-fifth of the need for lawyers among low-income people.

In this country, we presently spend $15 billion per year on legal fees for private lawyers in civil cases alone. Thus the Legal Services budget of $205 million a year is only about 1.3 percent of our national public and private expenditure on lawyers. That 1.3 percent must provide representation to nearly 20 percent of the population. Just by way of contrast, 13 percent of our national health expenditures, public and private, go for health care for low-income people (primarily through the Medicaid Program), as contrasted with the 1.3 percent spent on low-income poeple in legal matters. This means that we are ten times closer to meeting the health care needs of poor people than we are to meeting their legal care needs.

I also think we should remember that the problems Legal Services clients have are pretty much the same as the rest of the population. They need, as a result, more or less the same kind of help, not just help in divorce cases or support cases. Mr. Phillips suggested that Legal Services lawyers take so-called test cases (appellate representation is another way of talking about it) that somehow this is unique to the Legal Services Program, and that Legal Services lawyers should not engage in them. Let me tell you how these kinds of cases arise, from my own experience. When I was in the Washington, D.C. Legal Services Program, a young woman named Rosalie Jones came into our office with a problem common to a lot of people who came into that office. She had moved to Washington, D.C. just a couple of months before with her husband, who had since deserted her. She had no money and went to the Welfare Department for help. The Welfare Department said, "We're sorry, we can't help you. You have to live in the District of Columbia for a full year before you are entitled to welfare." I found out very quickly that she was one of a number of people who came to our office each week with that very same problem. Our choice was to continue to tell these people, "Sorry, we can't help you" or "Take the case up to the appellate courts and attempt to obtain a different reading of the law." In fact, the issue was taken to the appellate courts, and a few years later the Supreme Court of the United States did hold those residency requirements unconstitutional; thousands of Rosalie Joneses around the country were helped.

That is what a test case is. It is not some kind of insidious thing. Rather it is finally responding, after you have had the tenth or hundredth or thousandth client come to you with a problem where the law is stacked against them. It is pursuing a remedy in the appellate courts and attempting to obtain a new interpretation of the law that will be beneficial to your clients' interest. The alternative is to condemn the poor to illegal laws, deny them equal justice, withhold remedies from them that the affluent have all the time, and in a real sense deprive them of political equality.

There also has been some criticism by Mr. Phillips of legislative activity. I think that all of us would recognize that the legislative process is now very complex, and that indeed you need legislative representation before the state legislature or Congress if you are going to effectively participate in that adversary process, which is very much like a court. The California Fair Political Practices Commission recently issued a report revealing that about $20 million per year is presently spent in California to provide legislative representation before the state legislature. This report also indicated how much lobbying there was by Legal Services lawyers on behalf of poor people compared to with other groups. Of that $20 million, $12 million was spent by business interests, $2 million by local governments, and $75,000 by Legal Services organizations. This means that of the amount expended on legislative representation in California, a grand total of three-tenths of 1 percent was spent for the poor. Does that sound like some sort of powerful lobbying monopoly threatening American society? Of course not! Legal Services lawyers are providing a very, very small voice for the poor in an important lawmaking process so that this country will not be run entirely by an elite. If we have something to be worried about in the lobbying area, it is the enormous sum—$12 million— being spent in California by the tiny but powerful business elite, *not* the infinitesimal amount devoted to expressing the viewpoint of over 4 million Californians, the poor and powerless 4 million.

What the Legal Services Program is attempting to do in the state legislature is very much in line with what lawyers do for other kinds of people in society. It is not some kind of evil thing, but rather it provides a voice in the legislative chambers that is an essential prerequisite of political equality for the poor.

The next real issue is whether there is a need for a structure independent of the executive to run this kind of program? We have already heard a recitation of the history of the development of the Legal Services Program. I should like to point out that the Legal Services Corporation was not an idea of the liberal left, or Marxists, or anyone like that; it was actually an idea spawned by the American Bar Association and President Nixon, with endorsements from a full spectrum of organizations in this society, from the right to the left. President Nixon actually introduced one of the initial bills to establish a Legal Services Corporation.

Why did this broad coalition support this kind of corporation, separate from the executive branch? Primarily because of constant harassment from both within and outside the government every time a Legal Services lawyer attempted to provide representation for a client whose position was not favored by some politician or some other powerful element in society. In California we had probably one of the classic examples of this kind of political interference when Governor Ronald Reagan unilaterally cut MEDICAL (the program of medical care for low-income people in California) by some $200 million. One of our Legal Services agencies— California Rural Legal Assistance—had a client who needed an operation that he was no longer going to be able to afford because of that cut. The lawyer filed a lawsuit on his behalf, and that particular $200 million cutback was found to be illegal by the California Supreme Court.

From that moment on, Governor Reagan was committed to stop the Legal Services lawyers in one way or another and to kill the Legal Services Program that had the temerity to attempt to stop him from doing illegal things to the poor. At one point, he vetoed the grant to California Rural Legal Assistance (CRLA), which was the organization involved in the case I just mentioned. There were hearings held by three conservative Republican State Supreme Court Justices from other states (which went on for months, looking into some 107 allegations of improper conduct levied by Reagan's office). These were the same kinds of allegations that Mr. Phillips made about the Legal Services Program in general (that they were organizing prisoner's groups, unions, and the like). That particular hearing ended, holding that there was no substance to the charges. In fact, these conservative Republican State Supreme Court Justices went on to say that the complaints contained in Reagan's report did not either taken separately, or as a whole, furnish any justification whatsoever for any findings of improper activity. The commission expressly found further that in many instances the report had taken evidence out of context, misrepresented the facts, and in so doing, the report had unfairly and irresponsibly subjected many able, energetic, and devoted CRLA attorneys to unjustified attacks upon their professional integrity and competence. And I submit that most of the charges levied today in this room by Mr. Phillips are of the same nature. And it is politically motivated charges like this and politically motivated interference like this that made the need for an independent Legal Services Corporation so apparent to so many.

The Legal Services Corporation is analogous to the Corporation for Public Broadcasting. And the rationale is similar. We do not want the government dictating what we are going to see on the air waves, and we do not want a particular administration, congressman, or governor dictating what kinds of cases are going to be taken and what kinds of arguments are going to be made by lawyers representing low-income people. I might add that President Nixon himself, in introducing that particular piece of legislation, indicated that professional independence was absolutely essential and that this was one of the reasons why he supported the concept of independence of legal services for the poor.

This brings us to one of the chief attacks mounted by Mr. Phillips. We must look at the Legal Services Corporation for what it is; it is not a policy-making organization like the Federal Trade Commission and other similar organizations. It is not deciding what taxes are to be paid or who is going to get what from government, nor is it regulating the marketplace. Rather it is an *advocacy* organization. Of course, it is representing one point of view, the point of view of the client. The choice is this: the client has his point of view expressed with government funding, or that point of view will not be expressed at all.

The advocacy function is a completely different function. The reasons that we want policy accountability to our elected officials in the case of ordinary government agencies do not apply in the situation of an organization that advocates. There the important accountability is to the people being represented, the low-income people of this country. This is what the corporation provides. It is dedicated in its entire structure in making sure that Legal Services lawyers exercise independent judgment and are bound by the Canons of Professional Ethics to represent their clients' best interests. And they certainly have. If we impose on the Legal Services Program and its lawyers the kind of accountability to politicians that Mr. Phillips suggests, as opposed to the accountability to clients guaranteed by the Legal Services Corporation, then we are not just denying poor people what they are asking for, we are denying their right to ask for it.

Mr. Phillips has suggested that there is an alternative way of going about all this. He has suggested that we establish a so-called voucher system, which compensates private lawyers who provide the representation. It is something that is called "Judicare," and it has several problems. For one thing, it is more costly, by three, four, or five times, than delivering legal services through neighborhood law offices. This will result either in a far more expensive program or much less legal assistance for the poor.

On the same budget, in fact, Legal Services is now conducting studies to determine if Judicare could be made more effective. I personally have advocated for a number of years a program that would combine the best of the present staff attorney program with the Judicare program. It is the client option mixed system. This program actually operates in Quebec province, Canada, where each client can choose between a staff lawyer or a private lawyer to handle his particular case. Interestingly enough, in Quebec, given the choice between staff and private lawyers, low-income people take about 85 percent of their cases to staff lawyers, particularly landlord-tenant, welfare, and consumer cases, where expertise in the legal problems of the poor is most important.

It also has been suggested by Mr. Phillips that we adopt the other basic feature of the Brock-Helms bill, which turns most of the powers of the Legal Services Corporation over to the states. There is a small irony here. This is precisely the idea suggested by the National Lawyers Guild in the 1950s as the way to administer a program of legal services to the poor in this country. At that time the right wing branded the idea communistic. I do not think it is communistic, but I do have other problems with this approach. It would amount, in effect, to local option injustice. State control also would create the opportunity to have too many restrictions placed on legal services at the local level, which would be a terrible problem for the poor and the quality of legal representation they receive. We have seen too many examples of this here in California (like the CRLA matter I mentioned earlier) to want to try that nationwide.

Mr. Phillips also questions whether Legal Services lawyers should represent prison inmates. In California, since prisoners have a constitutional right to representation in civil cases, I cannot see why Legal Services lawyers should not provide that representation.[4] Also, it has been said that Legal Services lawyers, being put in the drivers seat to the extent that they handle the cases, will advocate only what they, or their bosses, want. But look at the Legal Services Corporation charter and the Canons of Legal Ethics. You will find that Legal Services lawyers provide representation free of interference from the corporations' board and are as duty bound as any lawyer to follow the client's request and serve the client's best interests.

To summarize briefly, we have confronted two major issues: first, is what Legal Services lawyers do good, and is it something that should be continued? I argue that it is providing political equality to the poor. In order to provide political equality, it is essential that Legal Services lawyers be allowed to provide representation in appellate courts, in Congress, and before the legislatures, as well as in the trial courts. The Legal Services Program has been doing all this very well. The effect of this kind of political equality is some redistribution of income, but that is inherent in giving a voice to the poor in the forums where it matters. The second issue addressed is whether an independent corporation is a sound way of administering the Legal Services Program. I argue that the Legal Services Corporation provides independence from political interference. This is essential because of the past history and continuing threat of political interference with the work of Legal Services lawyers. Thus, to both fundamental issues in this debate, the answer is a resounding yes.

Howard Phillips's Rebuttal

I would like to quote a liberal publication, the *New Republic*: "Lawyers naturally always have been the loudest supporters of Legal Services. . . . [Legal Services Corporation] funded programs offer jobs that otherwise wouldn't exist. . . . While siphoning off some of the overflow from the nation's law schools, the legal services program represents no competitive threat to private attorneys. . . . The beauty of creating a demand for lawyers by offering them "free" is that for every poverty lawyer who starts or threatens litigation on behalf of a client, at least one more lawyer (and possibly more) will be needed to represent the other side."[5]

Richard Cloward, who has been on the board of directors of a legal services back-up center, which played an instrumental role in the creation of welfare rights organizations around the country, argued that a great many more people were eligible for public assistance than applied for it. He recommended that more people get on welfare, in order to create a political and fiscal crisis which would spiral from cities to the states, forcing mayors and governors to lobby for federal assistance to meet the crisis. His plan (to overload the welfare systems and lead to a Socialist breakthrough in this country) became the master strategy of the National Welfare Rights Organization. And assistance to welfare rights chapters across the country by the legal services program was a major factor in their growth.[6]

The Legal Services Manual, the "Reggie" manual, named for the Reginald Heber Smith fellowship program, which is an effort to bring young law school graduates into the legal services, firmly stated its goal as "providing communities with assistance in organization and politicization of the issues." Desired qualities in Legal Services lawyers include "commitment to the goals of the program and commitment to reformation of certain institutions affecting people in poor communities." Professor Johnson's former colleague, Gary Bellow, stated that specific discussion with clients about political choices in the handling of their cases is far more likely to empower and educate them than continuing the myth that their causes are being resolved by an apolitical body of rules within an apolitical system.

It would be difficult to estimate the cost of suits brought by Legal Services against the U.S. government. Legal Services has been involved in a number of these kinds of suits. I would guess that it has certainly been in the billions of dollars. Professor Johnson's statement that legal aid services costs only $205 million is incorrect: a budget proposal was made for next year in which the cost will exceed $300 million. I would argue that $300 million for legal services is a very significant amount, since whether it is in the courts, lobbying, drafting legislation, initiating test cases, or whatever, it is influencing the public policies of the nation without recourse to the political process.

I think that one of the real dangers that we confront in our society is that we are increasingly defining one another in class terms rather than in individual terms. The Legal Services Program approaches the problems of people who are without economic resources as if there were an inherent class identity and an inherent class solution. I think that the essence of the American system is the way representation is based on geography and the total being, not on class identification. There is an essential difference between an individual seeking a cash remedy and stating that there is a class interest in being poor.

I do no believe that the government has an obligation to subsidize legal representation. I do believe that the government has an obligation to ensure equal access to governmental processes. I do not believe that it is the function of government to require the citizen to subsidize someone else's legal representation, because when you do that, people will use it even when you and I might conclude that it was unnecessary, because it is free. The absence of economic constraint in going to court leads to excessive litigation and excessive resort to the courts for disputes that can be resolved outside the court. I believe that any person with a legitimate grievance and a legitimate need for representation would be able to find a professional willing to provide representation. I believe that there are lawyers who can be found who will have genuine compassion, who would represent people who require professional representation, but I think the so-called need for professional representation is greatly exaggerated in this society.

The fundamental argument remains that he who pays the piper calls the tune. I would like to close with a quote from Thomas Jefferson: "[T]o compel a man to furnish contributions of money for the propagation of opinions which he disbelieves and abhors is sinful and tyrannical. . . ."[7] On that basis, the present Legal Services Program is sinful and tyrannical.

Earl Johnson's Rebuttal

In his argument against the Legal Services Program and the Legal Services Corporation, Mr. Phillips has tried to bring out a parade of horribles, of terrible things that have been said or done. We find that the Legal Services Program is a job program for lawyers, and for that reason we should not support the Legal Services Corporation. We should not provide needed legal help for low-income people because that would mean that there will be some more money for lawyers. I submit to you that we are talking about a very small part of what makes up the income of the legal profession of this country, and that has nothing to do with an on-the-job program for lawyers. It does not mean that the Legal Services Corporation is perfect or that the Legal Services Program is perfect. One of the parade of horribles that he conjured up was the problem of the small shopkeeper who is sued by Legal Services funded lawyers on behalf of a low-income client. This is indeed a problem, one that I addressed in my book *Justice and Reform*. We do not deal with that problem by denying justice to either side in order to avert injustice to one; what we do is make sure that there is justice for both, and we can fund the legal costs of the small businessman, similar to what is done in England. In this way, there is justice done for both sides.

We are also suddenly told of Cloward and Piven, who have recommended various things that have nothing to do with Legal Services. Yes, a lot of people sit on Legal Services boards, but not all are from radical dominated organizations. In San Diego, the boards are dominated by the local bar association, various local organizations, the public defenders office, and the prosecutors office. None of these organizations is committed to destroying this country, but rather they are all committed to ensuring equal justice by giving everyone, even the unpopular, a voice in the government of this society.

The question asked was the impact of Legal Services actions, how much does it cost? I do not know the figure either. I would also guess billions. But that is the legitimate effect of political equality, of giving people an opportunity to advocate their position. Legal Services did not decide to give $200 million for medical benefits or billions of dollars for food stamps; these decisions were made by elected officials, or by judges construing the law. If you give people a voice, it will be heard sometimes, and sometimes it results in more income for the voice, just as when a lawyer wins a case for a client and gets a money judgment or when veterans get more veterans benefits from the legislature.

I think Mr. Phillips is misled by the term *class action suit.* Class action suits are brought on the part of a class of people with similar interests. The Legal Services Program really has only one class, and that class is composed of people who cannot afford a lawyer to represent them where lawyers represent people. If Mr. Phillips believes that anyone in this country can get a lawyer to represent him without cost, he has a good case for a good defense. I submit that there is generation after generation of jurist, from Charles Evans Hughes to Lewis Powell, who will testify that this is not the case, that you need government subsidized representation or people will go without help.

It is not a choice between providing legal aid to the poor through a corporation or through vouchers. Legal Services can use any one of a number of ways of delivering services, including a voucher. I would prefer the Quebec-type plan, where the client has a choice. With regard to comparative costs, there are several reasons why the staff program can deliver the services for less (at $25 per attorney hour, as opposed to $50 or $60 an hour for private attorneys). First, staff lawyers are committed to helping poor people. Second, they are more organized and spend less time on each case because of their expertise on legal problems of the poor, which would not be developed if the work were spread throughout the bar.

I would also like to close with a quote from Thomas Jefferson, who in his first inaugural address said, "All . . . will bear in mind this sacred principle that though the will of the majority is in all cases to prevail, that will, to be rightful, must be reasonable; that the minority possess their equal rights, which the equal laws must protect, and to violate which would be oppression."[8] I submit to you that to deny low-income people the kind of services that are provided by Legal Services, and the kind of services that

could only be rendered to them if they have a politically insulated corporation, would, in fact, be oppression.

Notes

1. *The Adams-Jefferson Letters,* Lester J. Cappon, ed. (Chapel Hill, N.C.: University of North Carolina Press, 1959), p. 388.

2. Geoffrey C. Hazard, Jr., "Law Reforming in the Anti-Poverty Effort," *U. Chi. L. Rev.* 37 (1970):253–254.

3. Earl Johnson, Jr., *Justice and Reform: The Formative Years of the American Legal Services Program* 2nd ed. (New Brunswick, N.J.: Trans-action Books, 1978).

4. Payne v. Superior Court, 17 Cal. 3d 908, 553 P. 2d 565, 132 Cal. Rptr. 405 (1976).

5. Stephen Chapman, "The Intellectual Poverty of Legal Services: The Rich Get Rich, and the Poor Get Lawyers," *New Republic,* September 24, 1977, p. 10. Reprinted by permission of *The New Republic,* © 1977, The New Republic, Inc.

6. Frances Fox Piven and Richard A. Cloward, *Regulating the Poor: The Functions of Public Welfare* (New York: Pantheon Books, 1971).

7. 2 *The Papers of Thomas Jefferson,* (Julian P. Boyd, ed.) (Prince-ton, N.J.: Princeton University Press, 1950), p. 545.

8. 3 *The Writings of Thomas Jefferson,* (Washington, D.C.: The Thomas Jefferson Memorial Association, 1905), p. 318.

7 Government: Hindrance or Help in the Cancer War?

Elizabeth M. Whelan and
Ellen Haas

Elizabeth M. Whelan's Presentation

It is not surprising that Americans today are concerned about the safety of the food supply. In recent years we have been inundated with reports about potential hazards resulting from toxic chemicals in foods. We have heard that hamburgers may cause mutations, food additives turn our kids into speed freaks, nitrates, instead of referring to cheap telephone service, are potential killers, and potato chips belong on the FBI's public enemies list. No doubt when confronted with all this good news we feel like having a good stiff drink. But watch out, scotch might be a carcinogen too.

One factor that epitomizes American cancerphobia is the Delaney Clause of the Federal Food, Drug and Cosmetic Act. I think I am safe in saying that no aspect of the food safety laws has done so much to confuse the public about cancer, yet done so little to reduce our cancer burden. And there is little doubt that the National Academy of Science report on food safety had the Delaney Clause in mind when it stated, "The law has become complicated, inflexible, and inconsistent in implementation. Although complex in itself, the law is inadequate to meet the changing and increasing problems of food safety."[1]

I would like to focus my remarks on the Delaney clause and two of the more recent controversies it has helped to create: saccharin and nitrites. By using these examples, I hope to show that in at least these cases the Delaney Clause has hindered rather than helped the reasonable assessment of food safety.

The Delaney Clause, created as part of a legislative package known as the Food Additives Amendments of 1958, currently requires "that no additive shall be deemed to be safe if it is found to induce cancer when ingested by man or animal, or if it is found, after tests which are appropriate for the evaluation of the safety of food additives, to induce cancer in man or animal."[2]

It is difficult to estimate the total impact the Delaney Clause has had in preventing the addition of carcinogenic chemicals to foods. Petitions for new additives that are found to have carcinogenic activity are simply withdrawn before the Food and Drug Administration (FDA) can make a formal judgment. Some proponents of the clause suggest that this deterrent function is its most valuable asset.

But another measure of the Delaney Clause's effectiveness is the number of times it has been used to support regulatory action. Since 1950, when the threat of cancer from food chemicals became a national concern, the FDA has banned or otherwise restricted twenty food additives on the basis of carcinogenicity. Yet in only seven of these cases did the FDA explicitly invoke the Delaney Clause. In the other thirteen cases, the agency relied on the more general requirement of the law, which demands that additives must be shown to be safe. And in the three decisions made before 1958, the FDA cited the authority of Section 402, which prohibits adulterated foods containing poisonous or deleterious substances.

The Delaney Clause is a public-policy decision based on a conservative approach to the scientific uncertainties about cancer. It implicitly accepts animal models as reliable indicators of human cancer risk. And once a risk is identified, it limits regulatory options to a single course: complete and absolute prohibition. It is therefore a policy statement that will accept nothing short of zero risk for food additive safety. But let me stop for a moment and make a few comments about animal testing before going on.

There is no doubt that in the current state of affairs we must rely heavily on animal experiments to evaluate potential cancer risks. On the one hand, it is often difficult to obtain sufficiently sensitive data from epidemiological studies of food additive use, and ethical constraints prevent us from testing new chemicals directly on human subjects. Short-term tests, on the other hand, are too new and have not been extensively validated. Animal tests, in contrast, have been around for a long time; hence, there is a fairly good body of knowledge to draw from, and when managed properly, animal testing is a reasonably accurate qualitative predictor of potential human risk. But as valuable as they are, animal tests are far from perfect.

The most obvious limitation is simply that laboratory animals, particularly rats and mice, are not little men. Although they share some of the characteristics common to all mammals, there are substantial differences between rodents and humans in physiology, metabolism, and resistance or vulnerability to a given chemical agent. Rats, for example, manufacture their own supplies of vitamin C, while we must obtain this essential nutrient from foods.

Another sensitive issue, and one with which you are no doubt familiar, is the question of test dosages. Despite certain industry protestations to the contrary, high-dose testing is a scientifically valid procedure in most cases. These high doses are needed to overcome the statistical limitations of using a small number of test animals and the short lifespans of test species. But there is a point at which the dose becomes so high that it poisons the animal and, in so doing, makes it difficult or impossible to determine whether an observed tumor is the result of the poisoning or the test substance itself.

The point I am trying to make is that the determination that a given chemical is or is not a carcinogen depends almost entirely on the exercise of scientific judgment. And this judgment, in turn, depends on the evaluation of the complete body of evidence collected, not merely on the results of a single animal test.

The Delaney Clause, in my view, places too many restrictions on this need for judgment. While it allows for discretion in deciding whether a test is appropriate and allows some latitude in evaluating the results of a specific test, it denies scientists the authority to place these results in a perspective that is meaningful to human experience. The clause does not allow, for example, scientists to evaluate differences in metabolism between animals and humans. It demands action even if a rat or mouse metabolizes a chemical in a completely different way from that of human beings. Neither does the clause allow for the differential analysis of a number of studies. It again demands action if a test is positive in one strain of mouse, yet negative in rats, dogs, or monkeys.

But let me get back to the concept of risk, particularly the zero-risk philosophy of the clause. Our societal concept of acceptable risk varies from case to case. In the abstract, acceptable risk reflects our perceptions of ourselves in relation to our environment, but more practically, acceptable risk reflects our trust in technology to minimize or control various hazards as they arise. We have different levels of trust and thus different levels of acceptability, depending on whether a risk is perceived as voluntary or involuntary.

Because we need food for survival, we must assume a certain amount of involuntary risk. Yet, for the most part, the choice of specific food products to consume is a personal one, and so a voluntary act. We can choose to eat meat, or choose not to; our survival does not depend on any one specific element in the food supply. But it does depend on our ability to choose from a variety of food sources.

The Delaney Clause applies only to those food chemicals labeled as food additives. It has no direct authority over naturally occurring toxins, additives that were sanctioned prior to 1958, unavoidable environmental contaminants, or those ingredients which are generally recognized as safe. Because of these loopholes, the FDA can permit aflatoxin, described as the most potent liver carcinogen known, in corn, peanuts, and milk. Similarly, the agency ignores the natural estrogenic content of meats and vegetables, but is forced to act on DES implants.

In a word, the Delaney Clause is inconsistent, and perhaps dangerously so. Our bodies do not particularly care what regulatory label we attach to a food or food chemical. They simply react to its presence.

I would now, as promised, like to turn to my two examples, saccharin and nitrites. A brief summary of these should effectively point out some of the limitations of the Delaney Clause most clearly.

Saccharin, as you are no doubt sick of hearing, is the artificial sweetener the FDA most loves to hate, or regulate. Saccharin has been around for 100 years, and humans have tasted it in everything from Diet Pepsi, to chewable vitamins, to toothpaste. Saccharin has been the object of more than twenty long-term animal tests since 1950, yet in all but the very last, evidence of its cancer causing potential has been negative or inconclusive. However, in 1977, Canadian researchers detected what they believed to be a statistically significant relationship between saccharin consumption and bladder cancer in men. But they also came up with the curious and unexplainable finding the women who used saccharin are somehow "protected" from bladder cancer. Further analysis showed that the alleged risk was associated only with tabletop use of saccharin, not with saccharin-containing foods or diet sodas. And the most interesting finding was that for men who were lifelong nonsmokers or smokers of less than fifteen cigarettes a day, there was no risk at all.[3] It makes you wonder whether they were studying the effects of heavy cigarette smoking on bladder cancer, an association that is known to exist. The medical journal *Lancet,* in which the study was published, seemed to agree. The editors wrote, "Most readers will find the case against saccharin unimpressive."[4]

The nitrites issue presents some similar problems, but I should note that neither the FDA nor the Department of Agriculture (USDA) has as yet taken any formal action to ban nitrites.

Nitrites are among the oldest known food additives, although their specific action was not identified until the beginning of this century. Under the right (or if you will, wrong) conditions, nitrites can combine with other food chemicals called amines to form compounds known as nitrosamines. These chemicals are potent animal carcinogens, strongly suspected by some as human carcinogens as well. However, the joint FDA/USDA proposal to ban nitrites was directed exclusively at cured meat products. But here again, the myopia of the Delaney Clause influenced the regulatory judgment. If we accept, for the sake of argument, that nitrites themselves are a cancer risk, what then do we do about the other sources of nitrite exposure? Virtually every green vegetable contains a substantial amount of nitrates, which can be reduced by bacterial action to nitrites. And scientists have also recently discovered that the human body produces its own reservoir of nitrites and circulates them in the saliva. In fact, a recent study has estimated that nitrites from cured meats account for less than 5 percent of the body's total daily exposure to nitrites. But vegetables and saliva are beyond the control of the Delaney Clause, and here again is another example of the inconsistent approach to food safety that it perpetuates.

One point that I have not mentioned yet, but which is currently very fashionable, is the tradeoff between a chemical's risks and benefits. The perception and acceptability of benefits, like the acceptability of risk, is a

matter beyond the strict bounds of science. Many individuals are quite willing to accept the nerve-soothing benefits of a cigarette against the certain
risk of lung cancer. So too does our society accept the benefits of freely
available alcohol, despite the fact that there are more than 10 million alco-
holics in this country. In both these cases, we have refrained from exercising
regulatory choices on the grounds that these are individual voluntary
choices. But is the choice to drink a diet soda or eat a ham sandwich any less
voluntary or any more hazardous? How many people can we say have died
as a result of saccharin or cured meats?

I hasten to point out, however, that the perception of benefits is very
much in the mind of the beholder. And for this reason, benefits are exceedingly difficult to evaluate. Saccharin is a good example. It is reasonable to
assume that a zero-calorie sweetener should be an asset to those millions of
Americans trying to lose or maintain weight. But as the National Academy
of Sciences and many others have noted, there is no reliable data that can
support this assumption. It appears, then, that, like cigarettes, the benefits
of saccharin are largely psychological. But this should not be dismissed
lightly. Virtually every medical organization that has any interest in obesity
and obesity-related diseases supports the continued availability of saccharin
because it is an effective aid to patient management.

In the case of nitrites, the benefits are a little more clear-cut. Despite
testing more than 700 compounds, researchers have not been able to dupli-
cate the effects of nitrite as a meat curing agent. It appears to be unique in
its ability to preserve and color meats and at the same time lend a distinctive
flavor component. But its primary value is its ability to inhibit the growth of
botulism organisms.

The decision to accept or reject a food chemical based on a risk-benefit
evaluation is not an easy one, nor is it the exclusive function of scientists or
federal regulatory agencies. These are issues that must involve societal judg-
ments. And with that in mind, I would like to make some personal sugges-
tions for a change in our food safety law.

I believe that the basic principle of the Delaney Clause is sound. We
should limit cancer risks posed by food chemicals, whether natural or man-
made, to the extent feasible while still maintaining the quality and variety of
our food supply. But I think the rigid approach of the Delaney Clause needs
some modification.

The recognition that science cannot answer every question about cancer
or food safety does not, it seems to me, demand that we should automatically adopt an inflexible policy of safety evaluation. It would seem more
logical, when confronted by uncertainty, to keep open as many options as
possible. Effective regulation of food hazards depends on a complex analysis of many different factors, not a black or white, all or nothing, decision
model.

I would therefore like to see the Delaney Clause changed in two respects. First, I think the process by which a substance is labeled a carcinogen should depend on a complete evaluation of all available evidence, not solely on the results of a single animal experiment. In this way, those considerations which I noted earlier about metabolism and other interspecies differences would receive complete consideration. Second, I believe that there should be some recognition that absolute safety is unrealistic. I am not completely convinced that a formal risk-benefit process is currently feasible, but I think that the benefit side of an issue should not be automatically disregarded.

Like Congressman Jim Martin, who recently proposed modifications of the Delaney Clause similar to these, I am not in favor of a little bit of cancer. What I am in favor of is a little bit of common sense.

Ellen Haas's Presentation

Every year nearly 400,000 Americans die from some form of cancer. The second leading cause of disease-related death in this country, cancer is easily the most feared and the least understood. Cancer incidence, even after excluding those cancers clearly attributable to cigarette smoking, is on the rise, and despite the billions of dollars spent to find a cure for various cancers, science has come up against a solid stone wall.

Therefore, in recent years, somewhat greater emphasis has been placed on *preventing* cancer from striking. While scientists are not absolutely certain what exactly will cause a certain cancer in a certain individual, it is widely believed that many cancers are initiated or promoted through human exposure to one or more chemical stimuli. Thus when through careful analysis scientists identify a commercial chemical compound used in food that is carcinogenic, it becomes the responsibility of our government—which is charged with protecting the public health from hazardous food products in commerce—to remove or prohibit that chemical from food products whenever possible.

Obviously, the government may not be able to control *all* sources of exposure to a cancer-causing agent, but it does have complete control over *some* sources. Preeminent among this class of substances are those which the government sanctions for use as food additives. Current federal law recognizes the extent to which we can control the safety and maintain the credibility of our food supply by prohibiting the deliberate addition to food of chemicals that have been shown to be carcinogenic. In fact, food additives are unique in the sense that they are the only known cancer formers over which we do have complete control. If we do not add them to food products, they will pose no harm to us. This is the standard presently embodied in the Delaney Clause of the Food, Drug and Cosmetic Act. That clause reads: "No additive shall be deemed to be safe if it is found to induce cancer when ingested by man or animal, or if it is found, after tests which are appropriate for the evaluation of the safety of food additives, to induce cancer in man or animal."[5] And it is this standard that must be maintained.

However, there are some in Congress (and in society at large) who would like to neuter this law. The time has come, these interests proclaim, to update the food safety law from its last revision over 20 years ago. These detractors add that the Delaney Clause is antiquated in the face of what we now know.

On the contrary, my position is that this regulatory concept concerning food safety remains credible and justifiable from both the scientific and societal standpoints. Let us examine the reasons supporting this position. The first and most important is that even in 1979, serious gaps exist in our understanding of carcinogenesis. In particular, we cannot yet predict which exposure levels for *any* carcinogen might be safe for which groups of consumers, or even if this "threshold" concept applies to any cancer-causing agent. Moreover, the FDA has recently stated that "there is reason to believe that the classical toxicological concepts of 'threshold' and 'biologically insignificant' levels may not even apply to carcinogens and, further, that even if they do apply, there is no known method for establishing them in a manner that will provide the public health protection necessary."[6] Thus we must repeat today what was stated in 1958, 1969, 1970, and 1977: We do not know how to establish with any assurance a safe dose in a person's food for a cancer-producing substance.

The second reason is that although we can now detect very small concentrations of a particular carcinogen in certain foods, we cannot equate these smaller concentrations with lack of health significance. For example, aflatoxin, a carcinogen that occurs primarily as the result of improper drying and storage of grains and groundnuts, has been shown to cause cancer in all rats tested when fed in dietary concentrations of fifteen parts per billion. What is more, dioxin, a controversial component of some pesticides, was recently reported by former FDA Commissioner Kennedy as producing a significant adverse biological effect on test animals in concentrations of fifty parts per million. The fact that we can measure smaller concentrations does not in any way mean that these levels are harmless.

Third, scientists today cannot estimate with any precision the number of human cancers that will be caused by a chemical to which consumers are exposed. For example, estimates for the number of saccharin-caused bladder cancers reported in the National Academy of Sciences report on saccharin varied depending on the dose relationship and rodent-to-human statistical extrapolation model used from a low of 0.0007 cancers per 50 million persons exposed to a high of 3,640 cancers per 50 million persons—or a

5 millionfold difference. The committee concluded, in fact, that the cancer risk from saccharin could not be quantified or even roughly predicted.

Fourth, the fact that a carcinogen is present in small amounts does not mean that the carcinogen will have no effect on humans, and the statistical models that have been developed recently are useful only in assessing relative degrees of cancer-causing strength among animals tested. Moreover, although animal tests can identify which chemicals have the ability to cause cancer in humans, they cannot tell us how much cancer the chemical will cause. Thus the statistical models may be useful for purposes of study, but they cannot be relied upon as the basis for setting parameters to maintain the safety of the food supply; the argument that the rodent-to-human extrapolation model can be used to predict safe exposure levels for humans appears highly questionable. In fact, many believe that humans are much more sensitive to certain carcinogens than are experimental animals (who lead rather pampered lives), and more important, humans are exposed to many carcinogens almost daily—a situation that leads to possible synergy between natural and added substances. To the extent that we can eliminate some of the added substances, we can undermine this potential.

Thus even beyond the problems arising from attempts to calculate human risk from one carcinogen is the fact that many cancer experts believe that combined exposure to several different carcinogens is the principal route to cancer. According to an Office of Technology Assessment report on saccharin, "The total body of carcinogens is of greatest concern."[7] Any increment, even a relatively small one, to an already substantial burden of carcinogens must be taken very seriously. In fact Dr. William Liginsky of the National Cancer Institute has said that there is growing evidence that carcinogens act synergystically and that several experiments with nitrosamines, for example, have shown synergism.

The fifth reason for my position is that exposure cannot be confined to those who voluntarily assume a health risk. In other words, not everyone is able to make informed choices. Nevertheless, some critics of the Delaney Clause believe that the government should not attempt to protect the population from an unsafe food supply. They argue that consumers should be able to decide for themselves how much risk they are personally willing to assume. Let us explore this position carefully. Information about cancer risks could be distributed to the public on labels, in brochures, and through wide-ranging educational campaigns conducted by the government. But even if such a drive could be mounted, it is doubtful that it could ever approach the power of a number of effective advertising campaigns in terms of dollars or persuasion. Furthermore, certain portions of the population—children, fetuses, and the semiliterate—would remain unable to make informed choices. Even the educated and concerned in our society would have problems making such decisions. Only one who understands the complex concepts of experimental biology, epidemiology, and statistics would be truly capable of making a well-reasoned decision. In sum, the decision on whether to drink diet soda involves concepts (and variables of unknown magnitude) that are far more complex than those involved in the decision on whether to wear a motorcycle helmet. This position is supported by a Gallup Poll showing that only 24 percent of the American public believes that they had enough information today to make intelligent choices on cancer-causing substances in food.

In commenting on this situation, Richard Cooper, general counsel for the FDA, has said that "the general and strong presumption in food safety should be for protection and against [the concept of] freedom of choice. . . . People would rather spend their time and energy on the areas of life where freedom is really important and not worry about the toxicology of the food supply."[8] There is no reason in the world to require that people be food additive toxicology experts in order to shop; nor should we have to consciously consider cancer every time we enter the grocery store. That function properly belongs to the scientists at the FDA, and if they discover that a certain food additive may increase the potential for cancer, the American people deserve to know that it has been eliminated and that the overall potential for contracting cancer has been reduced.

My final reason for supporting the regulatory concept in the food safety area is that consumers should be free of unnecessary risk of disease. The presence in life of other risks demands the elimination of those hazards which are most controllable, especially when they entail involuntary exposure. Thus all certified carcinogens that appear in commercial products must be considered unsafe regardless of the concentrations in which they appear. That the American public wants this protection is evidenced by a 1978 Gallup Poll demonstrating that 59 percent favor banning all food additives used for cosmetic reasons. (Cosmetic additives, for example, give our hotdogs that beautiful brown-red color.) In addition, a 1978 Cambridge study done for Shell Oil Company, a chemical manufacturer, found that 72 percent of the public favored the Delaney Clause.

Recognizing this public sentiment, the government, which is charged with protecting the public health from hazardous products, has four policy options. First, it can treat all substances in food products equally regardless of origin and attempt a rank-and-regulate categorization in which the greatest cancer risks are regulated more strictly. Second, it can assess all risks posed to society from all sources and allow carcinogenic risks from food to equal an average value of risk from nonfood sources. Third, it can weigh the cancer risks of each substance against the benefits that such substance confers, prohibiting those substances whenever the former outweights the latter. Last, it can regulate most strictly the carcinogens over which it has greater control, including intentional food additives.

Let us look at these options one by one. The first assumes that we can actually quantify cancer risks posed to consumers by various hazardous substances. Although this quantifying might be possible for some categories of chronic risk (including allergies and food-borne poisoning, for example, when routes of hazard are more well known and epidemiological data are more complete), it is categorically impossible to quantify the risk of cancer from individual sources. Nevertheless, common sense tells us that this type of approach should be at least a part of the government's food safety policy.

The second option is ludicrous because (1) there is no way to equate food risks with nonfood risks, (2) the policy objective is to decrease risk, not allow all risks to rise to the level of the greatest risk to which we are exposed, and (3) consumers expect eating to be a safe and secure exercise; no one wants to experience the danger of riding a motorcycle without a helmet when she or he is eating a hot dog.

The third approach involves the application of a risk-benefit analysis in those instances in which a food additive is threatening. The concept is simple: when the benefits of a food additive outweigh the hazards, it is allowed to remain; when the hazards are greater, it is banned. But in practice it is not so simple. For example, given the limits in scientific understanding of how risk is quantified, we know of no safe doses; animal-to-human models are extremely crude at best and totally inapplicable at worst (we do not know which is closer to the truth), and we cannot predict synergy. Beyond all that, what is the value of one human life? Of 1,000 human lives? Can we willingly sacrifice any lives simply to enhance the color, flavor, or commerce of certain food products? In fact, how are benefits of food additives measured? How much weight should be placed on the psychological benefit to the consumer of seeing brightly colored soft drinks or the happiness of the diabetic teenager in being able to drink sugarless sodas at the corner store while other teenagers drink sugar-sweetened sodas?

Without controlled scientific studies concerning the benefit of food additives, attempts at quantification will reflect nothing more than advertising campaigns. This is particularly true in the case of saccharin. While many people believe that the chemical is useful in controlling weight or treating diabetes, no scientific evidence to that effect exists. Some animal evidence, in fact, suggests that saccharin actually increases appetite. But because the 18-year-long message to consumers about saccharin has centered on slimness and dieting, and because there has been no source of information to the contrary, the psychological perception of benefit (without scientific grounding) persists. Thus the third approach both confronts the problems of quantifying and categorizing food risks and is magnified by the virtual impossibility of developing a system for determining societal benefits from a certain food or food component.

An additional problem plaguing all three of these options is that they focus only on the known and measurable risks; they do not suggest a method for dealing with potential but unknown risks (either in identity or magnitude). Clearly, many food risks exist about which we know nothing or very little. Moreover, some carcinogens in the food supply were not added but rather occur naturally or are the result of inadvertent contamination. For example, one powerful carcinogen, aflatoxin, occurs regularly in improperly dried or stored grains and groundnuts. And DDT contaminates most agricultural produce today, even though spraying of that controversial pesticide was outlawed many years ago. Since we allow peanuts, corn, and a tremendous amount of other farm produce to be sold to consumers, the thinking goes, there is no reason to pick on a food additive if it happens to cause cancer in experimental animals.

But it is precisely because we are confronted with unavoidable carcinogens that we must act to eliminate those over which we have direct control. Again, total human exposure to all carcinogens is of critical importance. Because of this unavoidable exposure, we must act to reduce total body burden whenever possible.

Nevertheless, we should not overlook the identified carcinogens that occur naturally; to the contrary, we should make every effort to correct the production or processing problem that leads to contamination. For example, grains and groundnuts could be processed more carefully, or if that is insufficient, we should examine the question of whether certain products are genetically predisposed to the formation of the carcinogenic aflatoxin mold and whether that hereditary deficiency can be corrected.

In most cases, however, naturally occuring carcinogens and those resulting from inadvertant contamination of agricultural products cannot be removed, both swiftly and completely, from the food supply without eliminating the food itself from commerce. In the case of DDT contamination, this policy would obviously have unacceptable economic and dietary consequences. The same is true for aflatoxin-contaminated crops, albeit to a lesser degree. Because of these problems, we do not ban outright these carcinogens and their host foods. Instead we work to reduce total contamination toward the zero point. This approach is the one required by current food safety law. It recognizes the extent to which we can control the safety of our food.

With direct food additives, an entirely different policy is in order. Here if the additive is shown to cause cancer, we can eliminate it from the food supply or prohibit it from being used without incurring economic or dietary consequences anywhere near the magnitude involved in the naturally occurring or contaminant categories. In fact, there are already substitutes for most additives that have not been shown to be carcinogenic. In almost all cases, the additive in question can simply be dropped from the food supply with not so much as an economic murmur. Moreover, Congress decided long ago that no economic benefit was great enough to warrant the increased potential for cancer posed by the deliberate addition of a known carcinogen to food products. In a sense the existing law admits that while we cannot always eliminate the hazards Mother Nature throws down in front of us, we can prevent commercial interests from adding to that burden simply for purposes of financial gain.

Without a doubt, it is unconscionable for government to sanction the use of a known carcinogen in foods that we routinely consume in light of our professed scientific ignorance on the matter and the tremendous fear of cancer that permeates our society. Therefore, the fourth option is the only one acceptable today. Preventing such use is necessary from a scientific standpoint because it recognizes that which we do not know as well as the extent to which we can directly control the degree of carcinogenic risk in the food supply.

In sum, it is clear that the soundest food safety policy would combine our ability to eliminate the carcinogenic risks over which we exercise complete control and an attempt to reduce other, unavoidable cancer risks from foods on the basis of the magnitude of risk posed to the population. This guiding legal principle is as sound today as it was in 1958, when the Delaney Clause was enacted; in the intervening years, very little evidence has been presented that would credibly argue for its revision. We cannot say that the day will never come when the science of carcinogenicity is sophisticated enough to warrant changes in the Delaney Clause, but without a doubt, that day has not arrived in 1979. To make wholesale changes without having such an improved scientific foundation would inevitably lead to large-scale degradation of the safety and quality now characteristic of this nation's food supply. To eliminate the Delaney Clause or to require the use of statistical models in determining cancer-risk potential is to offer up the population to increased cancer incidence merely for the sake of food industry convenience and profit.

Elizabeth M. Whelan's Rebuttal

I think that we are dealing again with basic philosophy and human nature. People want other people to protect them from cancer. Early in this century you could turn to the government and say, "You protect us." This is how we got chlorine in our water. But the problem now is that the government cannot protect us from cancer, for it is our lifestyle that really has increased the risks. And of course, it is easier when you sit and watch the television to be screaming and yelling about saccharin and nitrites while you smoke your cigarette. It is more difficult to change your own lifestyle, so usually you ask someone else to do it for you.

However, I think that we have to agree that a society has to have some laws and regulations. When I walk into the supermarket, I do want to make sure that the food in there is safe by all current standards. But that is not the question here. Probably we all concede governmental ability to check restaurants, to make sure that poisons are not in foods, that food is not adulterated. But the question is now going beyond these functions; it is dealing with hypothetical risks. The question is eliminating substances that benefit us, that give pleasure to life and are responsible for our high standard of living—the food additives that keep our food supply safe, plentiful, and inexpensive. The government is crossing the line, and it is not protecting the public health in that sense. Rather, the government is again trying to get a zero risk for society at any cost. We do need things other than food safety in this world; we need food; we need clothing; we need energy. A lot of needs exist, and again we are back to the cost versus the risks involved.

The main problem that I see with the Delaney Clause is that it errs on the side of possible risks, for only one experiment is necessary to wipe out any other kind of evidence on an additive, as, for example, with saccharin. Twenty animal experiments have been done since 1950, nineteen of which either are ambiguous or show no cancer. A hundred years of use by Americans, decades of use by diabetics who consume enormous amounts of saccharin—all those data became irrelevant on March 17, 1977, when that Canadian experiment was announced. That one experiment dominated, and the ban was instigated. This is not common sense; this is overreaction; this is just plain dumb.

Thus the essential point is that we must measure benefit and risk. The fact that nitrites cause cancer in mice should not be conclusive. What about the benefits? How do you make that tradeoff? We have to sit down and make a decision on a chemical-by-chemical basis. We do not need a straitjacket. With nitrite the risk is hypothetical, but what are the effects of its ban? The most logical one that we all know about is botulism. However, consider also the economic implications of banning nitrites. If we cannot make bacon as we know it today, who is going to raise hogs? If we cannot sell hog bellies, the whole pork industry would be gone—a major source of protein in our diet would be gone.

With saccharin, Ms. Haas seems to be using any evidence from an animal experiment to put the additive into the category of known carcinogen, but I think that if we are going to be so specific about known carcinogens in talking about saccharin, we should get really specific. If we extrapolate to humans what we know from that one positive animal experiment, the only group at risk from saccharin would be male babies of women who drank enormous amounts of it during pregnancy, and only if those males themselves overdosed with saccharin throughout their lifetimes.

The implications of these things are absolutely enormous, and naively saying that nitrites cause cancer in an animal so we must ban them is purely unrealistic. When we are dealing with risks as hypothetical as saccharin and nitrites, I think that we should leave them in the freedom-of-choice category. If something were posing a risk, or even a good chance of a risk, I would not conclude that. I think that our government should have the power to ban risks when evidence exists. But here, right now, let us leave it to freedom of choice. If we intend to feed ourselves and perhaps some other portion of the world, we can do without some things, but we cannot continue the way we are. We cannot do without everything.

Of course we do have to test and regulate additives. However, no other country has a Delaney Clause or anything like it, and they all manage just fine. We can operate in a rational, scientific way by evaluating and making decisions on a chemical basis. We do not need a law dictating to us to ban something when event A or B happens. We have a general food safety law in this country, and the Food and Drug Administration, the food industry, and others are certainly not going to put something into our food supply that they have any strong suspicion, or moderate suspicion, is going to harm people.

Thus I am back to common sense rather than an arbitrary statute. I think that the problem is trying to get us all back on track about what causes disease and what the nutrition-related diseases are in this country. I do not want to cater to the fear that exists now by offering a law to people who think they are being protected by it when, indeed, it is only contributing to the cost of food. It is even worse than that. The Delaney Clause is in fact a disincentive for the food companies to come up with an artificial sweetener or anything else. Why invest millions of dollars in something when it could be banned?

This problem with the Delaney Clause centers on the legitimacy of animal testing—the natural versus artificial dichotomy—the entire concept of what causes cancer. I would like to reemphasize that I am not saying that animal experiments are not useful. If you showed me that saccharin caused cancer not only in a Canadian rat, but also in a dog or a guinea pig or monkey, or if you showed me some pattern, I would strongly urge our government to get that stuff out of our food. We do not need that kind of risk. Those data would be convincing to me.

However, such is not the case; we have one experiment that is in total conflict with the other available data. The National Academy of Sciences, in projecting the number of possible deaths related to saccharin, is using a purely mathematical model. There is no evidence to suggest that anyone develops cancer; projecting is something that statisticians do with their computers. The natural-versus-artificial dichotomy is something we really have to face. Why did we ban cyclamates in 1969 when vitamin A causes breast cancer in animals? This approach is simply inconsistent.

Epidemiology has taught us a lot in these last few decades. We have strong evidence that some aspect of our diet—excessive calories or high fat, we do not know—may explain why Americans have a high rate of breast, colon, and prostate cancer. I would like to see us paying more attention to the real things that pay off. If we are going to have a war on cancer, I suggest that we begin by identifying the correct enemy. What we see now because of the Delaney Clause is people avoiding saccharin in their coffee in the morning and then lighting up a cigarette. The clause is distracting us from research, and it is distracting us as citizens in planning our own preventive health goals.

Ellen Haas's Rebuttal

Apparently Dr. Whelan and I agree on one point: perhaps a war on cancer is necessary; perhaps there is an enemy. However, picking on the Delaney Clause is picking on the wrong issue. Remember that food additives are deliberately and intentionally put in food and that some additives do cause cancer. Are we then going to accept a policy that intentionally condones an addition to our food supply that is cancer-causing? And at the same time, are we going to continue to support millions of dollars in researching cures for cancer? The answer is that we need to form a policy of prevention.

Of course we cannot expect a food supply free of risk. The Delaney Clause never had as a goal a food supply free of risk; rather the Delaney Clause recognized our scientific limitations, recognized that some additives are cancer-causing, recognized the fear millions of Americans have about cancer. And it erred, if at all, on the side of caution, not for a riskless society, but for a reduced-risk food system.

As far as freedom of choice is concerned, I want to describe a scenario, created by Richard Cooper, who is now general counsel for the FDA. He imagined a freedom-of-choice supermarket. (Maybe this is what some people want, but it would not protect our health very well.) A warning over this super market reads "Abandon confidence in the food supply all who enter here." I know that somewhere inside are thousands of jars, cans, boxes, and substances that are risky but that were approved because they provide economic benefits to farmers and food processors. Others were approved because members of the public perceived them to be beneficial, although these benefits could not be scientifically demonstrated. Still others were approved to protect my personal autonomy, for which I thank the free-market philosophers. So now safety is something that I have to be concerned about along with quality and price. And that is exactly what will happen. Unless we have government regulation when it is needed, we will have that kind of openended anxiety and openended risk.

Thus the philosophical difference between Dr. Whelan's position and mine is that I strongly recommend that we make decision on facts, not on fears, and I accept that we cannot prove that something is safe. The phenomenon is contradictory; we can never prove safety. The only thing that we can do is look for harm, and when we cannot find harm, we have done our best.

In focusing on harm, the Delaney Clause states that if a substance is found to cause cancer in animals or humans (we are not doing human testing at the present time), that substance must be banned. Of course we cannot determine exactly how many cases of human cancer will result from a certain additive. And this point is one that I want to emphasize as true for all food additives and other contaminants. Unfortunately, when people die, we relate their deaths to particular agents; we do not relate deaths to additives. In fact, it is not possible to do so. Tests show whether someone died of bladder cancer, for example, not whether that person died of bladder cancer because she or he drank x amount of saccharin-laden diet drinks. Therefore, we cannot demonstrate a direct correlation. Again I am talking about a policy issue and a society judgment about where we want to place our values—on the side of risk or on the side of caution. My position is that although variance exists in experimentation, if scientifically valid experiments show that certain additives are cancer-causing, the law prohibiting their use in the food supply should be maintained.

Returning to the saccharin experiment, I want to reiterate that the National Academy of Science found, and no one disagreed with that finding, that those rats fed saccharin produced cancer. The original experiment with saccharin has undergone the most extensive review in history. It has been reviewed, and it has been evaluated, and it has been found valid. The system applied its checks and balances and its peer review, and the original experiment passed all tests.

If we are concerned about freedom of choice in this area, we can adopt the Canadian system. In Canada, where saccharin is banned in soft drinks, it is available as a "no-cal" sweetener that an individual can add to food. Thus the situation of involuntary exposure is taken care of. However, I am concerned about people who are not able to balance risks against benefits— if those benefits do exist. I am concerned, for example, about children who cannot read, who cannot understand labels.

As for the nitrite situation, we have one of the biggest growth markets in the food system today with no-nitrite bacon. For a long time it was not successful on the market because it had to be called "breakfast strips." But in the last month, the regulations have been changed, so we will see a swell of no-nitrite bacon. It is acceptable; it has recently been sold in a number of supermarkets, and sales have been high. And yes, if you want to keep that bologna sandwich for 4 weeks at 81°, nitrites will give you a preservative function, but we do not need nitrites in our bologna even for a lunch sandwich, even in 90° weather.

Moreover, just because we know that cigarettes are high risk, we cannot ignore additives that cause some risk. Yes, the Delaney Clause is limited to food additives. I ask, should we expand it? Should we include natural contaminants? Are its limitations reason to discard it? Or are they reason to explore the possibilities of extending the regulation?

As for expanding the clause to other diseases—cancer is considered a dread disease—the public policy is such that it places laws concerning the causes of cancer in a separate position. We do not have such laws for colds, for colds do not seriously affect the nation's health. However, the public has said, through its congressional representatives, that cancer-causing substances in our foods need to be regulated. Here the public has felt the need to be protected.

In contrast to this feeling, we are experiencing today a strong reaction against Big Brother and government, and I share this reaction in a lot of ways. I share this reaction in the case of economic regulation; I share it because our Big Brother, our government, sets our milk prices and our prices are much higher than need be for a nutritionally unequivalent product; I share this reaction in trucking because regulation causes our food prices to increase. However, I do not share this reaction in public health. This is not because I feel that Big Brother is going to do something for me, but when I eat, I want my food to be safe. I think that this feeling of protection is one shared by a good number of people, and I think that there is a difference between eating and picking up a cigarette, which is really a voluntary, knowing act.

Moreover, in the case of health services, the government is not controlling the flow of goods in the same way as with economic regulation. Economic regulation has only increased prices. It was never instituted to cut consumer prices. For example, milk regulation was established to protect the income of dairy producers, not to help consumers; not a word about consumers is written into the legislation. In this area there is unquestionably abuse of governmental power. There is lack of accountability. But this situation should not mean that we must throw out public health or consumer protection measures.

Dr. Whelan also stated that the Delaney Clause has raised the fears of the American public and that the Delaney Clause has been wantonly used. In fact, the clause has been seldom used. Of all the thousands of chemicals that have been studied, only 7 percent have been found to be carcinogenic. Only under the most extreme circumstances and with peer review and scientific evidence do we remove an additive from our food. The Delaney Clause, if it stays on the books, and the Food, Drug, and Cosmetic Act, if it is enforced the way it should be, simply will continue to be added protection in the form of prevention. The clause is neither overly important nor overly used, but it does protect the public health.

The tobacco industry is a good illustration of a laissez-faire situation allowing a vested interest—the tobacco lobby, which is as strong as they come—to influence governmental processes, to ensure that people keep smoking, to continue the subsidies to tobacco farmers. Advertising still exists; even though it does not exist on television or radio, it still exerts an impact on newspaper and magazine publishers so that articles may not include reference to tobacco-related health problems. Although the warning label also is used, cigarette use is going up. Tobacco could not be a sorrier or better illustration of what happens when a hugely flexible policy does not base itself on caution. If we were to change our food additive laws, we would open regulation of cancer-causing additives in food to the same political manipulation.

Because of fear, misunderstanding, misinformation, and the lack of ability to make sense out of the nonsense that is put forth, the American public today does not know what to believe. Therefore, we must have that which is being criticized as a rigid standard. A rigid standard in reality reduces anxiety and concern. If we were to leave the situation and open it to benefit-risk assessment, you can imagine the fear, you can imagine the anxiety, and you can imagine the increased incidences of cancer.

Notes

1. National Academy of Sciences, *Food Safety Policy: Scientific and Societal Considerations,* Washington, D.C., March 1979.

2. U.S.C. 21, Section 348 (c)(3)(A).

3. G.R. Howe and A.B. Miller, "Artificial Sweeteners and Bladder Cancer," *Lancet* 2, December 10, 1977, p. 1221.

4. G.R. Howe and A.B. Miller, "Bladder Cancer and Saccharin," *Lancet* 2, September 17, 1977, p. 592.

5. U.S.C. 21, Section 348 (c)(3)(A).

6. Food and Drug Administration, "Cancer-Causing Chemicals in Food Producing Animals" (Sensitivity of Method Document) March 20, 1979, p. 17070.

7. Office of Technology Assessment, "Cancer Testing Technology and Saccharin," October 1977.

8. *Food Chemical News,* June 25, 1979, p. 35.

Index

Index

List of Contributors

Harold Demsetz, Professor of Economics, University of California, Los Angeles

John Kenneth Galbraith, Professor of Economics, Harvard University

Jake Garn, United States Senator from Utah

Ellen Haas, President, Consumer Federation of America

Gary Hart, United States Senator from Colorado

Earl Johnson, Jr., Professor of Law, University of Southern California Law Center

Edward J. Mitchell, Professor of Business Economics, Graduate School of Business, University of Michigan

Howard Phillips, National Director, Conservative Caucus

Bernard H. Siegan, Distinguished Professor of Law, University of San Diego School of Law

Stephen J. Solarz, Congressman from New York

Donald T. Weckstein, Dean and Professor of Law, University of San Diego School of Law

Elizabeth M. Whelan, Executive Director, American Council on Science and Health

Lee C. White, Former Chairman, Federal Power Commission

Walter E. Williams, Professor of Economics, Temple University

About the Editor

Bernard H. Siegan is a Distinguished Professor of Law and director of law and economics studies at the University of San Diego School of Law. He is the author of *Land Use Without Zoning* and *Other People's Property* and the editor of *Planning Without Prices, The Interaction of Economics and the Law,* and *Regulation, Economics, and the Law* (all published by Lexington Books). He is also a contributor to professional journals and other publications, having written articles pertaining to land use and urban planning. Professor Siegan received the J.D. degree from the University of Chicago and was in private law practice for many years.